A Book Of
Exhortations

For Victorious Christian Living

Volume I

Gary Stafford

Changing Lives Publishing
Sharpes, Florida

Written by Gary Stafford
Cocoa, Florida

Published by Changing Lives Publishing
Sharpes, Florida 32959
www.Changinglivesbookpublishers.com

Printed in the United States of America

A BOOK OF EXHORTATIONS

For Victorious Christian Living

VOLUME I

Table of Contents

Pressing On.. 1

Deep Love... 3

Standing Watch... 5

Watchman... 7

Power... 9

Soldiers.. 11

They Came To Hear And Be Healed........................... 13

Great Exploits.. 15

The Fool... 17

Walking On Water.. 19

The Rich Versus The Poor... 21

Enter The Kingdom Of God... 23

They Shall Prophesy.. 25

Divine Providence.. 27

Prepare For Action.. 29

Do Not Shrink From Death.. 31

The Grace Of Jesus... 33

Do Not Harden Your Hearts.. 35

A Fire In My Bones... 37

My Word is Like a Fire and a Hammer......................... 39

Humility And Tears... 41

What Are You A Slave To?... 43

In Spite Of Strong Opposition..................................... 45

My Joy Knows No Bounds.. 48

Jesus Came To Destroy The Works Of The Devil........ 50

Take Heed What You Hear... 52

I Pursued My Enemy.. 55

Like A Flood The Spirit Of The Lord Will Lift Up A Standard............58

Where Sin Abounded, Grace Abounded Much More (1)................ 60

Where Sin Abounded, Grace Abounded Much More (2)................ 62

Restoring Grace... 64

The Lord Is Close To The Brokenhearted.................... 66

The Strongholds That Become The Accepted Norm..........................68

He Was Bruised For Our Iniquities... 70

Walk In The Spirit, And You Shall Not Fulfill The Lust Of The
Flesh... 72

The Spirit Yearns For Our Fellowship...................................... 74

Abundance Of Your House & River Of Delights.............................76

Given Over To Death For Jesus' Sake......................................78

The Test Of Our Love.. 80

Your Word Was To Me The Joy And Rejoicing Of My Heart........82

The Glory Of The Lord... 84

He Continues To Deliver Us.. 86

The Great Escape.. 88

Power In His Name... 90

What Do You Trust In?... 92

A Continual Feast... 94

Prayer.. 96

Prayer.. 99

Prayer.. 101

Prayer.. 103

Have You Received The Holy Spirit?.. 105

Why Tongues?.. 108

Where's The Power?.. 112

Be Filled With The Spirit... 114

Bold Prayers Get Bold Results... 116

Devote Yourselves To Prayer... 118

House Of Prayer... 120

An Expected End... 122

Mutually Encouraged By Each Other's Faith.............................124

How Strong Are You?... 126

You're Only As Strong As Your Weakest Link!............................128

Do You Love Me?... 130

Night Vision.. 132

But I Have Prayed For You!.. 135

Christ-Esteem... 137

"The Word Of The Lord Came To Me"....................................139

Persevere Under Trial... 141

Do Justly, Love Mercy, And Walk Humbly With Your God..........143

Jesus—The Light Of Life... 146

David And Goliath.. 148

Pride, Insecurity, And Rejection.. 150

The Prodigal... 153

Power Packed Scriptures.. 155

Mary's Famous Words.. 158

Do All In The Name Of The Lord Jesus...................................160

Are You Increasing?... 162

In All Your Getting, Get Understanding................................... 164

The Secret Things In Life... 166

Woman, You Are Loosed From Your Infirmity........................ 168

A Man's Heart Reflects The Man... 171

What Is The Lord's Will?... 174

If You Believe, You Would See The Glory Of God................... 176

Lord, Surely There Is A Stench!.. 178

What Is The Proper Response To God's Call?......................... 180

God Prepares Us For Changes In Life...................................... 182

Determination... 185

God Will Deliver.. 187

Safety Of Abiding In The Presence Of God............................190

Receive The Promise Of The Spirit Through Faith.................. 193

Drawing From The Wells Of Salvation................................... 195

Cannot Be Shaken.. 197

The Storm Before The Calm.. 199

In Christ Dwells All The Fullness Of The Godhead................202

Vision, Imagination, And Revelation....................................... 204

What Are You Pregnant With?... 206

Husbands And Fathers.. 208

Wine And Strong Drink.. 211

Neither Do I Condemn You; Go And Sin No More..................214

Servant Of All.. 216

Joshua's Orders.. 218

Introduction

The word exhortation in the Greek is "paraklesis". It means calling to one's side. A person that is called along side of you that will speak words of consolation, encouragement, and comfort. The person will also counsel and challenge you. An exhorter will urge earnestly and advise strongly.

Exhortation is a spiritual gift that is listed in Romans 12:8. An exhorter will use the Word of God prompted by the Holy Spirit to stir people into actions of faith and service.

This book is intended to spur you on in your faith in Jesus Christ, to challenge you to think and see according to God's perspective. It is also intended to bring salvation, healing, and blessing into your life.

As you read this book, I encourage you to read it in an attitude of prayer, listening to the Holy Spirit. Meditate on the exhortations, and ask God to give you application for your life. Allow your faith and vision to be stretched.

Gary Stafford

Acknowledgments

I want to express my love and thanksgiving to my lovely wife, Angela, who was so patient with my late nights. Thank you for your love, faithful support, and encouragement in writing this book.

To my Pastors, Jim and Jean Brissey: You have been my mentors, friends, and co-laborers in the work of the ministry of Jesus Christ. Thank you for all your support.

Also, to my other pastor and friend, Randy Alonso, thank you for all your encouragement.

I also want to thank Geoff Gill who helped with my editing. You were definitely a God send. Thank you for your support and encouragement.

And to my faithful intercessors, James and Victoria Boeseman, thank you for your prayers and encouragement.

Most of all, I thank God, my Lord and Savior Jesus Christ, and the Holy Spirit, for the divine inspiration and guidance I received while writing this book. To Him I give all the glory!

Gary Stafford

Pressing On

Philippians 3:12 (NIV) "I press on to take hold of that for which Christ Jesus took hold of me."

Questions to ponder: Am I steadily pressing on in Christ's call on my life? Have I become lukewarm, cold, stuck in a pit, or on fire? Am I hindering the Holy Spirit in any way, through outright sin and rebellion, doubt and unbelief, fear, or not being willing to step out in faith and take some risk?

When you think of the subject of risk, is it really a risk? Think about it—in Christ everything is always a win-win situation. The worst thing that can ever happen to us as Christians is death. And we know that to die is gain (Philippians 1:21). Even if someone rejects you in your witnessing, you still planted a seed. And it is not you they're rejecting; it is God.

In Matthew 5:10-12 (NKJV) Jesus said, "Blessed are those who are persecuted for righteousness' sake, for theirs is the kingdom of heaven. Blessed are you when they revile and persecute you, and say all kinds of evil against you falsely for My sake. Rejoice and be exceedingly glad, for great is your reward in heaven."

We see that these so called risks are centered around fear, doubt, disobedience, and selfishness. So precious saints, let the fire of God fall on you and run the race set before you with faith and perseverance. Burn with passion, which will only come from our consecrated prayer closets. We do not get passion from the recliner but from carpet time with God, on your knees.

Jesus said in John 14:12 (NKJV), "Most assuredly, I say to you, he who believes in Me, the works that I do he will do also; and greater works than these he will do." This Word challenges me never to be content with status quo Christianity. I am challenged to believe big, think with vision big, ask big, and to press on doing the Father's work. For He is great and awesome in me and through me. Freely we have received, so freely give. There's no greater joy than to walk in fellowship with God and to do what He has called us to do.

Remember that the DNA of God's call and gifting on your life is unique and different from everyone else's. Do not get caught up in the trap of comparing yourself with the anointing on others. We all have a special role to play in the kingdom.

So as I said in the beginning, it is time that we press on. Do not live in the past with regret and condemnation, do not live in the future with fear and anxiety, but live in the present in the abundant provision of His grace and power, which causes us to reign in this life as over-comers.

Take hold of that awesome call on your life and do not let go, like a pit bull with a t-bone steak. Once again the key to the passion and fire of God, and not letting go is that consecrated prayer closet. Let us continue to pray for one another. And remember that Jesus said, "The kingdom of God is to be forcefully advancing" (Matthew 11:12 NIV)!

Amen!!!

Deep Love

1 Peter 4:8 (NIV) "Above all, love each other deeply, because love covers over a multitude of sins"

The word "deeply" in the Greek means the stretched or strained muscles of an athlete. That puts a whole different emphasis on our actions of love. Are we loving to the point of being stretched or strained?

Looking at this emphasis on love will cause us to go to our knees in prayer, because none of us can love God's way without the help of the Holy Spirit. We know from Romans 5:5 that God's love has been put in our hearts by the Holy Spirit, but we still need to show our daily dependence on Him in all situations.

One of the ways to pray in order to love deeply is to say, "Holy Spirit I yield to you. I yield to love and all the fruit of the Spirit. I yield to your power. Have your way with me, in me and through me. Amen!"

So in reflecting on loving deeply, when was the last time that you were stretched in love? Remember in Luke 6:27-28 (NIV) Jesus said, "Love your enemies, do good to those who hate you, bless those who curse you, pray for those who mistreat you."

There was a time in my life that I was bound in bitterness toward someone that had hurt me. When I began to pray for that person, God softened my heart and set me free. Now, of course, they are not to be prayers of vengeance but prayers of forgiveness and blessing toward the person.

In 1 Chronicles 4:10 Jabez prayed, "enlarge my territory". Within that prayer, is the Spirit stretching us? In other words, "God enlarge my territory of influence and my capacity to influence." Isaiah prophesied to Israel in Isaiah 54:2-3 (NIV), "Enlarge the place of your tent, stretch your tent curtains wide, do not hold back; lengthen your cords, strengthen your stakes. For you will spread out to the right and to the left; your descendants will dispossess nations and settle in their desolate cities."

In putting this all together, if we want to live victorious in all things and take back from the enemy's camp, we have to be willing and submissive to the stretching of our love and faith muscles. Galatians 5:6 tells us that faith works by love.

The kind of deep love that Peter talks about is not blind love. It is love that sees and accepts the faults of others. As Paul said in Colossians 3:13 (NIV), "Bear with each other and forgive whatever grievances you may have against one another. Forgive as the Lord forgave you."

So let us get back to the gym of the Holy Spirit and do some serious stretching and get those muscles in shape!

Amen!!!

Standing Watch

Habakkuk 2:1-3 (NIV) "I will stand at my watch and station myself on the ramparts; I will look to see what he will say to me, and what answer I am to give to this complaint. Then the Lord replied: Write down the revelation and make it plain on tablets so that a herald may run with it. For the revelation awaits an appointed time; it speaks of the end and will not prove false. Though it linger, wait for it; it will certainly come and will not delay."

In ancient times watchmen were stationed on city walls to watch for any approaching enemy. The watchmen were not to sleep while on watch as they looked diligently. The prophet Habakkuk is taking this same approach with God as a prophet for the people. We can learn from the prophet's attitude to station himself and stand watch.

Being a watchman can be applied to all walks of life, whether as a parent, a spouse, clergy, schoolteacher, businessperson, politician, or government worker. It is all about stationing ourselves to hear from God. It is important that we all hear from God for direction into our lives. We need direction in our relationship with God and with people. We need direction for our churches, government and businesses.

We're not to compartmentalize our lives into secular and spiritual activities. Actually, everything in life is spiritual and God is to be at the center of everything. So stationing ourselves to hear from God is about the attitude of the heart, whereby you want to hear and you set aside that precious time to spend with God and seek His face. To seek the face of God is about worshiping and loving God.

In the atmosphere of worshiping God we will be drawn closer to Him and in that place we will hear from Him. As God spoke to Habakkuk saying, "write down the revelation and make it plain on tablets so that a herald may run with it", we too should get in the habit of journaling what God is saying to us. The fact that you keep a journal shows that you are diligent to hear and receive. God will speak to you in your Bible reading and studying, in your quiet times of prayer and worship, and in dreams and visions. Do not put off your dreams but tap into them. So we see, as with Habakkuk, so will it be with you and me. Station yourself to hear and receive. Write it down, and run with it.

We are called to be heralds of the Gospel and whatever God speaks to you; in one way or another, it will apply to God's purposes of His goodness in your life. More than ever before, we need people who are willing to stand their watch and seek God for a Word that will bring change and breakthrough, and who are willing to run with it. Those who are not willing to run with the Words that God gives, are those who will receive less and less from God. Eventually God will stop speaking and people will dry up.

Let us have the attitude of true intercessors as Isaiah 62:6-7 (NIV) says, "I have posted watchmen on your walls, O Jerusalem; they will never be silent day or night. You who call on the Lord, give yourselves no rest till he establishes Jerusalem and makes her the praise of the earth."

See, a true intercessor will not only pray but will also proclaim to the world. Herein lies the dual ministry of priest and prophet, which Jesus was both, and we are to do the same works as Him!

Amen!!!

Watchman

Habakkuk 2:1-2 (NIV) "I will stand at my watch and station myself on the ramparts; I will look to see what he will say to me, and what answer I am to give to this complaint. Then the Lord replied: Write down the revelation and make it plain on tablets so that a herald may run with it."

Here are some questions to reflect upon: Am I standing watch for my family? Am I crying out for God's grace and mercy for my family? Is my heart prepared to hear and receive from God? Am I taking the time to hear from God so I can minister to my family? Along with standing watch for my family, am I standing watch for the Church?

It is important that we take time to pray and minister to our family before we do so for others. Am I more content with watching television all the time and scanning the internet, more so than praying?

Have you lost your joy and passion? If so, get on the floor, prostrate, right now and begin to seek after God. God is calling all of us to stand watch. Are you heeding His call? Are you standing watch for the souls in the valley of decision? We cannot just pray people into God's kingdom. We have to pray and proclaim. Shout it from the house tops. Pray, go, proclaim, and pray some more. That is what being a watchman is about: watching God to hear and receive, and watching the people to pray and proclaim. When we watch people, we're being sensitive to what we see and hear about them, and then, hearing from God, we minister to them.

As Luke 19:10 (NKJV) says, "The Son of Man has come to seek and to save that which was lost." That is what we do as well when we're watchman. Of course we are not doing the saving, but the Holy Spirit within us does as we follow His leading.

Are you being faithful on your watch? Have you become complacent in your cozy life? Have you got so caught up in other things in life, such as sports and pursuit of material things, that you are thinking only of your agenda? Yet underneath all the fluff in life, when you get real honest with yourself, you know that you are unhappy and unfulfilled. Yes, standing watch can have its difficulties, but it is all in God's power, not your own.

The Apostle Paul was faithful in standing his watch to the very end. He too had many difficulties in life, but he tapped into the joy of the Lord. His joy had no limitations (2 Corinthians 7:4). That is how he continued to press on, just as Jesus did. Jesus endured all for the joy that was set before Him (Hebrew 12:2).

My friend, you and I are the joy that Jesus saw when he was going to the cross. As we see through the eyes of the Spirit, all the lives that will be changed because of our faithful watch, then we too will endure and overcome!

Amen!!!

Power

1 Corinthians 2:1-5 (NKJV) "And I, brethren, when I came to you, did not come with excellence of speech or of wisdom declaring to you the testimony of God. For I determined not to know anything among you except Jesus Christ and Him crucified. I was with you in weakness, in fear, and in much trembling. And my speech and my preaching were not with persuasive words of human wisdom, but in demonstration of the Spirit and of power, that your faith should not be in the wisdom of men but in the power of God."

Many will hinder themselves and God because of fear and weakness. We see clearly by Paul's example that God does not expect us to be a super strong saint when we first accept God's call on our lives. It is God's grace and God's Spirit that makes us confident and competent as ministers of the Gospel.

We all go through growing pains as we draw closer to God and must take baby steps as we do so. Growth and maturity in ministry is a process. In looking at Paul's example, we see that in the beginning of his ministry he felt weak, fearful and trembled, and he did not think his words were of any excellence of speech. But he still spoke! That is the important thing to understand! And His preaching came with power.

In the natural, many may feel weak and fearful prior to ministering in any situation, but once we begin to do what God has called us to do, the fear and nervousness will fall away. It is a matter of putting your faith in the Holy Spirit and not yourself. This is where prayer comes in – telling God that you trust and depend on Him.

If you are called to minister in speech, do not think you have to have everything on paper or stored in your head. Yes, we should study and be prepared and even have notes, but the most important thing is to learn to know the Holy Spirit. We want to be sensitive to His leading with ears to hear. Eventually you will get to a place where you are no longer nervous and you have complete confidence in the Holy Spirit.

In 2 Timothy 4:2 (NKJV), Paul tells Timothy, "Preach the Word! Be ready in season and out of season." In season is when you know you are getting ready to minister and you are prepared. Out of season is when opportunities pop up all of a sudden.

You might have an opportunity to preach on the spot with no notes, just trusting God. You might sense the Holy Spirit telling you to go pray with, prophesy or witness to someone. So we always want to be ready by being in prayer always and starting out the day in prayer and the Word. For me it is those spur of the moment type of opportunities that are powerful and exciting. Here again, you have to move past those feelings of fear and weakness and press through. The more you do it the more it is not even a concern.

When you get a thought, Word, prompting, or desire to do something, go with it and trust God. You will be amazed at how His power will flow through you!

Amen!!!

Soldiers

2 Timothy 2:3-4 (NIV) "Endure hardship with us like a good soldier of Christ Jesus. No one serving as a soldier gets involved in civilian affairs—he wants to please his commanding officer."

A soldier must first go through basic training before going to battle. In basic training a soldier will learn all the basic knowledge of what it means to be a soldier, along with learning how to do everything. There will be physical and mental tests to pass. The duress will get harder and harder as the training goes on. This is all for the purpose of preparing for battle. There are also different degrees of training based on what you are being trained to do. A Navy SEAL for example goes through the toughest training there is.

As Christians, we too must go through basic training to be good soldiers of Christ Jesus. So many say a prayer to get saved and then never go through any kind of Biblical training. Those are the ones who will struggle all through life.

Jesus promises freedom to those who will continue in His Word (John 8:31-32). That life of freedom consists of discipline – discipline to read and study God's Word, and the discipline of prayer.

Just as a soldier learns basic knowledge that has to be applied to his or her life, so we as Christians have basic foundational truths that we are to pattern our lives after. Just as a soldier must endure hardships, so must we. God has given us His Holy Spirit to be warriors not wimps. We are to have a voice of triumph within us, not a voice of crying and complaining all the time. Just as some soldiers will have specialized training, many Christians will also have specialized training. That is another reason why novices should not be ordained in ministry right away; training for ministry is much more than getting a degree.

In looking at my own life, I have endured many hardships and have gone through a lot of specialized training, but God's not done with me yet. Until the day we go home to be with God, we will have to endure many hardships and continue to go through training. A good soldier always stays fit and alert and continues to persevere.

Notice that Paul said, "No one serving as a soldier gets involved in civilian affairs." In other words, we are to stay focused and on the mission. We are not to get involved with things that distract us or pull us off the mission. That includes too many comforts in life, which lead to complacency. As a good soldier is focused on pleasing his commanding officer, remember that Jesus is our Commander in Chief, who we are to please.

The way we please Jesus is to walk by faith and not by sight and yield ourselves wholeheartedly to Him!

Amen!!!

They Came To Hear And Be Healed

Luke 6:17-19(NKJV) "A great multitude of people from all Judea and Jerusalem, and from the seacoast of Tyre and Sidon, who came to hear Him and be healed of their diseases, as well as those who were tormented with unclean spirits. And they were healed. And the whole multitude sought to touch Him, for power went out from Him and healed them all."

The reason why these people got healed was not because Jesus had the power to heal (which He does). They were healed because they came expecting to receive. They were thirsty to receive from God. That is the key element missing in many in our churches today. We have religion with tradition and ritual. We have beautiful cathedrals. But where is the thirst and hunger to receive? Where is the power to heal and deliver? God hasn't changed throughout history, but our thermostat for God has changed!

As I am typing this I am saying "God stir up your people. Let your fire fall". Not a fire of judgment, but a fire of desire, passion, and desperation. Church, we're not desperate enough! We want our ears tickled with a feel good message, not being challenged.

God wants to do more than heal our bodies and cast out devils. He wants our hearts consecrated unto Him so we can walk in wholeness, spirit, soul and body. The multitudes came to hear. Do you want to hear from God?

That should be our attitude everyday and every time we set foot in our local churches. Psalm 107:20 (NKJV) says, "He sent His Word and healed them, and delivered them from their destructions." If we're not ever hearing any Words on healing, how can we expect to receive? Romans 10:17 (NKJV) says, "Faith comes by hearing, and hearing by the Word of God." As long as we have medical insurance, a pill to take, and a credit card to use, why do we need God?

Where's the desperation that drives us to want to hear and be healed? Where's the desperation for us to want to be free from those tormenting evil spirits?

The crowds came touching Jesus in order to be healed. Today, the Church is the body of Christ and we can lay hands on the sick and see them recover, and we can come to one another expecting to receive.

We need to know that it is God's will for His people to be healed. We need to take the guesswork out of the equation and stop doubting God's power. It is all by His grace not by your works of righteousness, as Paul reminds us in Galatians 3:5.

So I encourage you to seek God and His amazing grace with all your heart. Stir yourself up in the Holy Spirit: seek to hear and receive. Once you are healed and set free, be a conduit of God's grace and power to minister to others.

God blesses us to be a blessing. Jump in the river of life and let the Spirit flow!

Amen!!!

Great Exploits

Daniel 11:32b (NKJV) "But the people who know their God shall be strong, and carry out great exploits."

Now that is a mouth full! If only this were the theme that all the Church lived by.

Jesus said in John 17:3 (NIV), "Now this is eternal life: that they may know you, the only true God, and Jesus Christ, whom you have sent."

To know God speaks of intimacy, like the sexual union of a husband and wife. So to know God means you have a personal and intimate relationship with Him. God is like the air you breathe. You seek Him first and always, everyday. You are in constant communication with Him. You are sensitive to His leading and promptings.

To know God means that you know His character and power. God's character is love and grace. Grace is all about God giving to us as a free gift. Anything and everything that comes from God to us is a gift of His grace. Grace is all of God's goodness, love, favor, power, intervention and blessing that comes to us on the merits of Jesus Christ and not on our merits.

To know God is also knowing His Spirit and how He works within us and through us. So to know the Holy Spirit we need to have a relational knowledge of the fruit of the Spirit and the gifts of the Spirit. We need to learn to know the voice of the Spirit. The voice of the Holy Spirit will always reflect what the Word of God says. There will never be any contradiction between the two.

To know God begins with you inviting Him into your life. You do that by believing that Jesus died for your sin and rose from the grave, and confessing with your mouth that Jesus is your Lord and Savior (Romans 10:9-10, 13). How much you know God is not about how old you are in the Lord, nor about how much head knowledge of the Bible you have. But it is about spending time with Him learning and growing with that constant desire to be intimate.

I know many men do not like the thought of intimacy when it comes to God. That sounds too mushy and emotional; that's for women more so than men. Men, if that is your natural tendency to think or feel that way, turn from that thinking. Remember, Jesus was a man, and God used men to write the entire Bible. These were men that knew their God and they did great exploits.

Before we can do great things in the name of God, we must first know Him! And in knowing Him we become strong. Then out of that strong place we will do great exploits. An exploit is a daring act, a bold deed, or to make use of. When we think of making use of, we need to make use of our time, living wisely, because the days are evil, and Jesus is coming back very soon.

A daring act could be witnessing to someone for the first time. It could be stepping out of our comfort zones with some radical faith. A daring act might be going up to a stranger to pray with him or her, or going up to a stranger to say God has given me a Word for you. A bold deed might be confronting someone of some sin in his or her life. A bold deed could be approaching a crowd on the street and sharing the Gospel. A bold deed is simply living your life of faith without fear and with strong conviction.

So, as I have already mentioned, if we are going to do great things in the name of God, it begins with knowing Him. In order to know Him we have to spend time with Him, which means thirst and hunger after Him. When you thirst you will drink, and when you continue to drink in the life and power of the Holy Spirit you will live the strong life, thus reflecting true boldness!

Amen!!!

The Fool

Luke 12:13-21(NIV)

Luke 12:15 says, "Watch out! Be on your guard against all kinds of greed; a man's life does not consist in the abundance of his possessions." From there Jesus tells a parable of a certain rich man who had an abundance of crops. That rich man built a big barn and filled it with all his grain and goods. The man said to himself, "You have plenty of good things laid up for many years. Take life easy; eat, drink and be merry." But God said to him, "You fool! This very night your life will be demanded from you." Jesus continues the story and says, "This is how it will be with anyone who stores up things for himself but is not rich toward God."

Recently a cable technician came to my house to do a repair. While he was here I said, "Is there anything I can pray for you." His response was, "No. I'm doing good in life." I replied back, "So you're telling me that you don't need God's help with anything in life." And again he said, "No I'm good." My response to that line of thinking is "Lord have mercy!"

From there I then asked him if he knew whether he was going to heaven when he dies, and he did not know. So I shared the Gospel and gave him an opportunity to receive God's free gift of salvation, but he declined. The attitude of this cable technician seems very similar to the fool in the story.

No wonder Jesus said in Luke 6:20 (NKJV), "Blessed are you poor, for yours is the kingdom of God." It seems like the more we have the less we need God, or so we think. But in reality everyone needs God as much as the next person.

It is obvious that our money and material things, or pursuit thereof, do get in the way of a healthy relationship with God. No wonder so many people in third world countries are more receptive to the Gospel, and more receptive to the miraculous power of God.

The sad reality is that many in the Church fall into the same trap that the rich fool had fallen into. The Apostle Paul gives a great commentary on this subject in 1 Timothy 6. He said, "Some people, eager for money, have wandered from the faith and pierced themselves with many griefs." (1 Timothy 6:10 NIV). Just look at how many people trust in their portfolios more so than they do in God.

Money can be here one day and gone the next. Or natural disasters can devastate a community. But those who have God in their lives will be sustained in such difficult times.

In the parable of the rich man, the most important questions for all of us to ponder are: Am I ready to go meet my maker? Is my soul saved or lost? Am I living to help get people saved?

I close with Jesus' Words in Matthew 16:25-26 (NIV), "For whoever wants to save his life will lose it, but whoever loses his life for me will find it. What good will it be for a man if he gains the whole world, yet forfeits his soul? Or what can a man give in exchange for his soul?"

Amen!!!

Walking On Water

Matthew 14:22-33 (NKJV)

In this scripture we read that Jesus was walking on water coming to His disciples, who were struggling to row the boat due to a storm. In verse 28, Peter said, "Lord, if it is You, command me to come to You on the water." Jesus replied, "Come" and Peter got out of the boat and walked on the water to go to Jesus. We then read that Peter began to sink after he first walked on the water.

I would rather be a wet water walker than a dry pew sitter. How many of us are willing to get out of the boat? We talk about the power of God and we even teach about the power of God, but what evidence is there of any power in our lives?

Too often we are ready to speak of reasons to doubt more so than of reasons to believe. Too many in the Church today has put God in a box. Man, bound in a spirit of religion, tries to set the parameters of what God can and cannot do. There are so many moves of the Holy Spirit that are new and different to the average pew sitter, and we are afraid to challenge and stir one another on to higher ground.

The Apostles would not be welcomed to minister in most churches today. Why is that? If we believe in the Book of Acts, we need to know that those acts are still viable for today as well.

Notice that Peter said to Jesus, "Command me to come to you on the water." The Bible gives us many New Testament commands on how to live the Spirit-filled life. Also, if we listen we will hear the Holy Spirit giving us many commands to go and minister to specific people in specific ways. The more we actually get out of the boat the more power we will see released, the more joy we will experience, and the more fulfillment we will have in life.

Many times we do hear God speaking, and then we ask for a dozen different confirmations. Come on people, all those signs we are asking for to confirm a Word is just us trying to squirm out of His will. God will not play that game very long. Those who are serious about getting out of the boat, they will walk on water. Everyone else will just dry up like prunes.

I do not know about you but I do not want to be a dried up religious prune. I want to walk by faith and not by sight. I want to lay hands on the sick and see them recover. I want to witness to people and see them get saved. I want to minister freedom to the oppressed. I want to hear the Spirit and prophesy with accuracy. I want to have dreams and visions and see them fulfilled. I want my cup overflowing with joy and love and a powerful anointing.

Remember what Jesus said in John 4:34 (NKJV), "My food is to do the will of Him who sent Me, and to finish His work." And in John 20:21 (NKJV), "As the Father has sent Me, I also send you."

The Spirit is calling you and He is sending you. Will you heed the call and get out of the boat?

Amen!!!

The Rich Versus The Poor

Luke 16:19-31 (NKJV)

In this parable, the rich man had everything good in life, but he did not have God. The poor man had everything bad in life but he had God.

Sometimes that becomes a struggle to figure out why life is so. The writer of Psalm 73 had this same struggle. It became oppressive to him when he tried to understand. Psalm 73:17 (NIV) says, "till I entered the sanctuary of God; then I understood their final destiny."

We all must face death. And whether you are rich or poor, healed or sick, does not change your destiny after death. What decides our destiny after death is what we did with Jesus while we were living. There are rich people that are believers in Jesus Christ and there are rich that have rejected Jesus. There are poor people that are believers in Jesus Christ and there are poor that have rejected Jesus Christ. So we see that being rich versus being poor has transcended unto all, whether you are a believer or not.

Being spiritual does not automatically equal prosperity. The scriptures that stand out to me on this subject are Ecclesiastes 5:12 (NIV), "The sleep of a laborer is sweet, whether he eats little or much, but the abundance of a rich man permits him no sleep." And Ecclesiastes 6:1-2 (NIV), "I have seen another evil under the sun, and it weighs heavily on men: God gives a man wealth, possessions and honor, so that he lacks nothing his heart desires, but God does not enable him to enjoy them."

You see one person works hard and sleeps good but another person, though he is wealthy, works too hard and is stressed and anxious all the time, and gets no sleep. Also, even though a sinner has prospered, and appears to enjoy his wealth, deep within he still has no peace or joy. That is a grievous and meaningless life.

1 Timothy 6:6 (NKJV) says, "Godliness with

contentment is great gain." What matters most is that your heart prospers in relationship with God, and that your finances, whether much or little, should be used for the work of God's kingdom. Does that mean that you should not try to improve your financial life as a Christian? By no means. You can be content and at the same time strive to improve yourself. Being content is all about the attitude of your heart while you are going through different phases in life. In other words, you can still operate in love, peace and joy no matter what phase of life you are in. Being content also means not being jealous, angry, and bitter toward others that might have more than you.

In Philippians 4:11-13, Paul tells how he has learned to be content, whatever the circumstances. His secret to contentment was that he could do all things through Christ who strengthened him. He meant that rich or poor, hungry or well fed, the grace of Christ is always sufficient for every circumstance.

So remember the key to contentment, and that your final destiny is the most important factor in life!

Amen!!!

Enter The Kingdom Of God

Mark 10:17-27 (NIV)

The main theme of this scripture is the rich man asking, "What must I do to inherit eternal life?" and Jesus' final response to His disciples, "With man this is impossible, but not with God; all things are possible with God."

When Jesus said that with man, inheriting eternal life is impossible, the Word of God confirms that again and again. On the part of man, eternal life does not come by our efforts of good works. Ephesians 2:9 and Galatians 3:1-5 point that out. Eternal life does not come by religious traditions. Matthew 15:6-9 makes that clear.

Based on what Jesus said in Matthew 7:21-23, even praying a particular prayer of salvation does not necessarily get you into the kingdom of God. I know that might burst the bubble of some Evangelicals. I am all for getting some one to pray a prayer of salvation. That is how I got saved.

Everyone that is truly saved prays something from the heart when salvation first becomes real. But the sad truth is that many will pray a coached prayer and never experience any change of heart.

As Romans 10:9-10 points out, we need to believe in the resurrection of Jesus and confess with our mouths that Jesus is our Lord. This happens as The Spirit enlightens our hearts to believe in Jesus Christ as our Savior.

In John 3:5-6, 6:40 and 6:44, we see that it is only by the Spirit that we get saved. In Romans 12:3 we see that God has given us a portion of faith to believe. This comes by the Holy Spirit speaking to our hearts about the truth of the death and resurrection of Jesus, and the eternal life that comes as a result of believing on Jesus Christ.

Believing in your head all the right facts about Jesus does not get you saved. James 2:19 (NKJV) says, "You believe that there is one God. You do well. Even the demons believe and tremble." When we look at the word "believe" in the Greek language, it entails trust and commitment, which is much more than just believing in your head. John 1:12 (NKJV) says, "But as many as received Him, to them He gave the right to become children of God, to those who believe in His name." This verse speaks of receiving Him in a personal way as your Lord and Savior.

Something else that is important to see on salvation is that it begins as the seed of God's Word is planted into our hearts (1 Peter 1:23). And a seed takes time to germinate. So let us not be quick to judge anyone's salvation.

Going back to the main text in Mark 10, verse 21 says, "Jesus looked at him and loved him. 'One thing you lack', He said, 'Go sell everything you have and give to the poor, and you will have treasure in heaven. Then come, follow me.'" We see here that Jesus was not looking for any kind of prayer or ritual response from the man, but He wanted his heart. Wealth had the man's heart and Jesus knew it. Once Jesus has our heart then we will truly follow Him. That is what real salvation looks like.

Does anything or anyone have your heart other than God? 2 Chronicles 16:9 (NKJV) says, "The eyes of the Lord run to and fro throughout the whole earth, to show Himself strong on behalf of those whose heart is loyal to Him." Is your heart loyal to Jesus Christ? Are you following Him in a committed relationship? Do you confess Him as your Lord in public? Is there enough evidence stacked up against you that you are a follower of Jesus Christ?

Salvation starts with grace and will bear the fruit of good works!

Amen!!!

They Shall Prophesy

Acts 2:16-18 (NKJV)

On the day of Pentecost after 120 souls were filled with the Spirit, Peter quoted these verses from the Prophet Joel. God had said that He will pour out His Spirit on all flesh and they shall prophesy. So what does it mean, "to prophesy"?

You are a spokesperson and mouthpiece for God. When the Holy Spirit comes into you as a believer in Christ, you now have the capacity to hear the Holy Spirit speak. The Holy Spirit will speak to you from the written Word of God, from dreams and visions, and during your prayer and worship times.

When the Holy Spirit speaks to you it is called "Rhema". Rhema is Greek for the spoken Word of God, spoken to your heart. When the Holy Spirit speaks to you it may be for your growth. It may be an attitude or behavior you need to look at. It may be a Word of wisdom for your life, or some direction about some decisions to be made. It also could be about a particular work of ministry God wants you to do. Now when the Holy Spirit speaks in regard to ministry, it could be a seasonal ministry, or an ongoing ministry. Or it could be a Word in the moment to minister on the spot to someone.

I said all this as some groundwork for hearing. We need to be able to hear from the Holy Spirit in our own lives before we start hearing for others. When the Holy Spirit speaks, it is not a loud audible voice, but it is like a still small voice. Sometimes it seems like it is coming from our own thoughts. That is common since 1 Corinthians 6:17 (NKJV) says, "But he who is joined to the Lord is one spirit with Him." So in other words, many times when the Holy Spirit is speaking, it is in the form of first person more so than third person. Also His speaking can come in the form of a prompting or stirring of your spirit.

In regards to prophesying in the New Testament, here are a few scriptures to know. Revelation 19:10b (NKJV) says, "For the testimony of Jesus is the spirit of prophecy." So Jesus and His grace needs to be at the core of what you are saying to people. Also 1 Corinthians 14:3 (NIV) says, "But everyone who prophesies speaks to men for their strengthening, encouragement and comfort." So as the Holy Spirit leads us to speak, it will be to build people up—not tear them down. In Romans 12:6b (NKJV) as Paul was speaking on spiritual gifts he said, "If prophecy, let us prophesy in proportion to our faith." We see that faith is important when speaking.

When we hear from the Holy Spirit, that Rhema Word will impart faith to us and to those we speak. Sometimes there will be a stretching of our faith by the Holy Spirit. The more we flow in the gift of prophecy, seeing and hearing more for the people, the more faith will also be at work within us. Prophecy can flow with the teaching gift, evangelism, and with gifts of healing. Prophecy will also flow in worship and in counseling.

What I enjoy within this gifting is when God gives me a Word for a stranger or when I am praying over people and God gives me a Word for them. Many times where faith comes in, are at those times when you hear only one Rhema Word at first, but as you are faithful to speak that Word, others will flow with it.

In 1 Corinthians 14:5 Paul wishes that all would prophesy and in 14:1 he encourages us to desire to prophesy. So in view of Paul's encouragement and Joel's prophecy, I too encourage you to desire to prophesy and yield to the in-filling of the Holy Spirit. The Church needs to operate in power in order to see lives healed, set free and changed.

Will you jump into the river of life and be one of God's prophets?

Amen!!!

Divine Providence

John 4:3-42 (NKJV)

This scripture records Jesus traveling from Judea to Galilee. The journey went from the south to the north, with Samaria in between Judea and Galilee. There was a great hatred between the Jews and Samaritans. There were deep racial, cultural, and religious differences. So usually the Jews would avoid Samaria by traveling out and around the city in order not to have any interaction with the Samaritans. But on this day Jesus had to go through Samaria because of God's divine providence for a special visitation with an outcast woman.

This speaks volumes of God's love and concern to reach people that are in desperate need. I have seen first hand how God's providence works, just like this. Simply put, this means that God sends a person at a special time in their life to minister to someone in need. The person in need to receive this special invitation from God may not always be receptive, even though God showed up. But the important thing is that God showed up and the seed of God's Word was planted and the impression of His Spirit was felt.

In verses 6-7, we see that Jesus was tired and thirsty from His journey, and this caused Jesus to go to the well for a drink. Sometimes God uses our circumstances to bring us to that place of using us for His divine visitation to someone. It could be any kind of trial that you are going through, even a flat tire, or an appliance needing a repair. What's important is that you are sensitive to the leading of the Holy Spirit and not getting upset about any inconvenience in life. As 1 Thessalonians 5:18 (NIV) says, "give thanks in all circumstances, for this is God's will for you in Christ Jesus." As we have that attitude of thanksgiving in every situation in life, with a yielded heart to be used by God, we will witness many powerful demonstrations of God's providence. Remember that a delay in your schedule could be part of

God's schedule to minister to you or to use you in ministering to others.

Notice from Jesus that He simply asked the woman for a drink. We do not want to come out with both barrels blazing giving the answer of Jesus to life's problems. But we want to be sensitive to people's needs and take time to get to know them.

That one question of simply asking for a drink opened a big dialogue for Jesus to share eternal life and to get to the core of the woman's pain. Her pain was centered on having 5 husbands and now living with a man. She was probably an outcast in her community, with much shame. Once the woman was receptive to Jesus as the Christ, she ran to town to tell others. They too then came to hear Jesus speak for 2 days and they received Him as well. All because Jesus had to go through Samaria, a whole community was changed!

Will you be sensitive to God's divine providence? Will you submit to God's leading and timing in your life regardless of your circumstances or inconveniences? Let that be part of your daily prayers. "God, I submit and yield to you this day no matter what comes my way. I yield to your leading and timing in everything. May I be sensitive to you, Holy Spirit, with seeing eyes and hearing ears. In Jesus' name".

To God be the glory!
Amen!!!

Prepare For Action

1 Peter 1:13a (NIV) "Therefore prepare your minds for action; be self-controlled."

When a sentence starts with the word "therefore" it is always a continuation of thought from the previous sentence or chapter. In 1 Peter chapter one, the previous verses are talking about our glorious and joy-filled salvation, which the angels desired to look into. Since we have such a glorious and joy-filled salvation, Peter is telling us to prepare our minds for action.

Because we have such an awesome salvation that brings forgiveness, cleansing, healing, deliverance, protection, provision, prosperity, and all of God's goodness and favor, we have reason to tell others the good news. Since it is such good news to the souls of man, the devil will try to deceive and steal and destroy what we have from God. The devil opposes everything that represents God and His goodness. Therefore, we have all the more reason to prepare our minds for action.

When you prepare to do something, you are getting your mind ready and you are thinking about the task. Preparedness also coincides with "pre-prayer". There is no better way to prepare for any task than to do it by prayer. As we pre-prayer we are expressing our dependence upon God.

Our prayer time gets us filled with the Holy Spirit. As we are filled with the Holy Spirit we will be filled with love instead of hate, peace instead of turmoil, joy instead of despair. We will have power, strength, authority, confidence and boldness. Preparedness also consists of meditating on God's Word. The Word and the Spirit flow together within you creating faith. When your faith is strong, you will speak with confidence and boldness without fear. Faith is voice activated, so as you speak you are building yourself up as well as others.

Remember that meditating on God's Word is also

speaking it out loud to yourself. This is all part of preparing your mind for action. Also, as you pray and worship, listen with ears ready to hear what the Holy Spirit might say to you as part of your action plan. There will be different actions every day in accordance to God's leading.

In 1 Peter 1:13 it also says, "be self-controlled". In the Greek language it means to be free from every form of mental and spiritual drunkenness or excess. Believers should be directed and controlled from within by the Holy Spirit instead of being controlled by outside circumstances. Spiritual drunkenness could be any kind of demonic oppression, deception, or obsession. We want to live our lives always prepared. We do not want to be in denial of any form of weakness. We want to live with our spiritual eyes and ears wide open.

Be accountable to friends in Christ and speak into one another's lives. As you live your life in accordance to this command, you will advance God's kingdom within you and on earth. Are you up to the challenge?

May the Holy Spirit spur you on to preparedness with a ready heart to go higher and higher in Him!

Amen!!!

Do Not Shrink From Death

Revelation 12:11 (NIV) "They overcame him by the blood of the Lamb and by the word of their testimony; they did not love their lives so much as to shrink from death."

Revelation 12:10-12 is a picture of Christ's followers who died living out their faith and are now in heaven. One of the absolute keys to powerful living is not being afraid to die, living life to the fullest in Christ. That is why Paul encourages all believers in Christ to offer their bodies as living sacrifices, which is our reasonable act of worship (Romans 12:1). But the enemy to this kind of powerful living is the dynamic fleshly trio: me, myself and I.

As Christ followers, it is important to die to self and all of its lust and affections. We read in Galatians 2:20 (KJV), "I am crucified with Christ: nevertheless I live; yet not I, but Christ liveth in me: and the life which I now live in the flesh I live by the faith of the Son of God, who loved me, and gave himself for me." Also in Romans 6:11 (NIV), "In the same way, count yourselves dead to sin but alive to God in Christ Jesus."

Notice Galatians 2:20 says, "We live by the faith of the Son of God". The same faith that was in Christ is in us by the Holy Spirit, but it is not an absolute faith that takes over our lives; we have to yield to it. As we yield, this is the kind of faith that denies self, and takes up it is cross daily. The cross is a picture and reminder of death. So, here again we are reminded to die to our selves and put God and others first. This faith in Christ is death defying, unshakeable, and immovable. When you live your life in that kind of faith, you will always respond to God's calling with an astounding "Yes Lord, here I am. What do you want me to do?"

Going back to Revelation 12:11, they overcame the devil and were not afraid to testify because they did not love their lives so much as to shrink from death. The stronger our love is towards God, the less we will have a selfish love toward ourselves. When you have died to self and you are not afraid of death, then you would not back down from the devil or any obstacle he brings your way.

Excuses why we do not yield to God's call are simply a reflection of a fearful and selfish person. But we do not have to remain in that place of isolation, boredom and oppression. We can break free from the prison in which we are bound. It is for freedom that Christ has set us free (Galatians 5:1). Jesus came proclaiming freedom for the captives (Isaiah 61:1). Jesus said in John 12:24 (NIV), "I tell you the truth, unless a kernel of wheat falls to the ground and dies, it remains only a single seed. But if it dies, it produces many seeds."

So the question is: are we only thinking of ourselves, like a lonely isolated kernel of wheat? Or, are we thinking of God's call, getting our focus off of self and our fears, being willing to die to it all in order to see a harvest of souls and fruitfulness, and thus living our lives to the fullest?

Amen!!!

The Grace Of Jesus

Matthew 12:20 (NIV) "A bruised reed he will not break, and a smoldering wick he will not snuff out."

This verse is part of a Messianic prophecy from Isaiah, chapter 42. This verse speaks volumes of the grace of Jesus Christ in action.

"A bruised reed he will not break." Jesus was bruised for our iniquities and chastised for our peace (Isaiah 53:5). Jesus gave His life and bore all the sorrow and pain in exchange for us to receive healing and wholeness. So He is not going to go against what He died for.

When we are bruised from the consequences of sin, whether it is our sin or someone else's sin against us, Jesus says, "Come to Me and find rest for your souls." (Matthew 11:28-29). When we are bruised from demonic oppression, we can know that Jesus heals the oppressed (Acts 10:38). When we are bruised from sickness and affliction, we can know that Jesus sends His Word to heal (Psalm 107:20). When we are bruised because we have been rejected again and again, know that He was rejected in order for us to be accepted and set free.

Picture a bruised reed in your mind. It is like a life that is down and discouraged, rehearsing the lies of condemnation. When we are bruised, we think that God cannot or would not use us any more. Then, because of the cross of Jesus Christ, the Holy Spirit comes alongside us to help lift us up, to encourage and empower us.

Know this: Jesus will in no way stomp on you and destroy you. He will nurse you back to vibrant life. He will send people to love you, encourage you, pray with you and help you.

"A smoldering wick he will not snuff out." This is a picture of our light that has gone dim. Whether the light has gone dim due to our sin or the sin of others, is not an issue of judgment but an issue of forgiveness and restoration. Yes, we need to repent from sin and confess it, and we need to forgive others of their sin toward us, but make sure you do not get stuck at pointing fingers. "Mercy triumphs over judgment!" (James2:13 NIV).

The smoldering wick is a picture of someone rejected and wounded, trying to hold on to their last ounce of hope. Every step forward is met with two steps backwards. Maybe it is someone that keeps hearing the voices from the past saying, "You're worthless, you're a nobody, you're pathetic and you will never amount to anything." Those demonic voices keep tearing away your hope and diminishing your light. Then Jesus comes on the scene. Instead of snuffing out your smoldering wick, He gently blows on the coals of your heart. Fresh wind and fresh fire from the Holy Spirit. Jesus keeps blowing gently and before you know it you are healed and set free and your life is now a fireplace for the glory of God!!!

Now go and do likewise for others. Freely you have received, freely give!

Amen!!!

Do Not Harden Your Hearts

Psalm 95

This psalm starts out with a call to worship in verses 1-3 and verse 6. "Come, let us sing for joy to the Lord; let us shout aloud to the Rock of our salvation. Let us come before Him with thanksgiving and extol Him with music and song. For the Lord is the great God, the great King above all gods." "Come, let us bow down in worship, let us kneel before the Lord our Maker." Then, in verses 8-11, the Psalmist warns Israel not to harden their hearts as their fathers did in the desert.

It is very interesting to see the difference of thought, going from worshiping the great King to a warning, not to harden their hearts.

God knows that the heart of man is deceitful above all things, and desperately wicked (Jeremiah 17:7). So it makes perfect God sense to see the flow of thought in Psalm 95.

In John 2:23-25, Jesus would not entrust Himself to many that believed because He knew what was in their hearts. In Mark 4:16-17, Jesus explains that many receive the Word with gladness but when times of persecution and tribulation come they fall away because the Word of God was not deeply rooted in them.

We see through out the Bible that God says, "Man worships Me with theirs lips but their hearts are far from Me." The Apostle Paul prophesied in 2 Timothy 3:1-5, that in the last days people will be lovers of pleasure rather than lovers of God. They will have a form of godliness but denying the power of God.

The prophet Amos also talks about the complacency of man in Amos chapter 6, where they have a prideful and self-righteous attitude, with religious ritual but no heart after God or His people.

So the lesson in all of this can be seen in Paul's words in 1 Corinthians 10:12 (NIV), "So, if you think you are standing firm, be careful that you do not fall!" Psalm 95:8 (NIV) says, "Today, if you hear His voice, do not harden your hearts."

It is easy not to harden your heart when every Word you hear is a sugar coated, pie in the sky, type of Word or that God loves everyone and there is no hell or any kind of judgment. But in God's love, He will speak hard and difficult Words to us, such as repent and confess your sins, check your attitude and motives, and "deny yourself, take up your cross daily and follow me".

In James 1:18-25 we are reminded to receive the Word of God humbly with a teachable heart. The fathers of Israel, which Psalm 95 is referring to, tested God with their complaining and murmuring and quarreling with Moses (Exodus 17 and Numbers 20:1-13). In the wilderness, Israel had seen God's power and miracles but they still hardened their hearts.

To prevent a hardening of the heart, it is important that we respond to God immediately when He speaks and not delay. Delayed obedience is disobedience! There is a special anointing of the Spirit in the proper responding time. The longer we delay and disobey the harder our hearts will become. When our hearts get hard, we become dull of hearing and we open the door for demonic strongholds.

So, today if you hear His voice, do not harden your heart. Instead, respond in faith and obedience, and worship God with all your heart as the great God and King!

Amen!!!

A Fire In My Bones

Jeremiah 20:9 (NIV) "But if I say, I will not mention him or speak any more in his name, His Word is in my heart like a fire, a fire shut up in my bones. I am weary of holding it in; indeed I cannot."

We see from Jeremiah a very descriptive picture of the Word of God being alive within him. In Jeremiah 23:9 (NIV) God says, "Is not My Word like a fire." In 1 Corinthians 9:16 (NIV) Paul says, "Yet when I preach the gospel, I cannot boast, for I am compelled to preach. Woe to me if I do not preach the gospel." In Paul's and Jeremiah's writings we see an overwhelming compulsion within them to preach the Word of God. This compulsion to preach is there because of the call of the Spirit on their lives and because the Word of God is spirit and life.

When the Word is planted in you and germinates, it starts to produce the very life of God flowing out of you. Within that life of God comes a strong desire to proclaim the Gospel. 2 Corinthians 5:14 (NIV) says, "Christ's love compels us." The love of God is what fuels the fire of the Word of God. Romans 5:5 (NKJV) says, "The love of God has been poured out in our hearts by the Holy Spirit who has been given to us." The more we yield to the Holy Spirit in our lives, the more we yield to God's love. The love of Christ that compels us is a love from God, towards God, and through us to others.

So when we preach, it is because of love, not of any kind of secret and judgmental agenda. Jeremiah wanted to stop preaching because of all the persecution that was coming his way, but he could not stop because that Word was alive within him. He could not contain it. I completely understand because the Word of God is also shut up in my bones like a fire. I want to share God's Word whenever, wherever, however and to whomever.

As we yield to the leading of the Holy Spirit everyday, we want to be sensitive for opportunities to speak. As a preacher of the Gospel, I encourage all preachers not to hold back with that compelling call. There's no place for timidity. We are called to be fearless ambassadors. Preaching is not just for the pulpit on Sunday mornings, but throughout life. Make your own pulpit on the streets and in the market place, by the leading of the Spirit.

When the Word of God is shut up in your bones like a fire, it is like a volcano that is ready to erupt or a pressure cooker ready to blow steam. It is because that fresh Rhema is brewing and stirring within you.

Once when I was getting ready to preach at a retreat, a brother prophesied over me saying, "I see the Word of God ready to come out of you like fiery Frisbees. As you speak, the Word will go into their hearts, as if you're throwing those fiery Frisbees, and them sticking in their hearts." I say praise God to that!

That is another vivid picture of what the Word of God and Spirit of God are doing within you as you have a Word to preach. We always have a Word to preach if we listen to the Holy Spirit and are spending time with Him. That is why Paul said in 2 Timothy 4:2 (NIV), "Preach the Word: be prepared in season and out of season; correct, rebuke, and encourage—with great patience and careful instruction."

So I encourage all to press on and proclaim the Word that God puts within you. Do not let yourselves become stagnant but stay in the current flow of the Holy Spirit!

Amen!!!

My Word is Like a Fire and a Hammer

Jeremiah 23:29 (NKJV) "Is not my Word like a fire?" says the Lord, "And like a hammer that breaks the rock in pieces?"

The Word of God is the real refiner's fire. The more the Word burns in us, the more the Word will burn out of us. John the Baptist mentions in Luke 3:16 that Jesus will baptize with the Holy Spirit and fire. The Spirit-filled life consists of being filled with the Word of God too. As Colossians 3:16 says, "Let the Word of Christ dwell in you richly." The Holy Spirit and the Word of God is what refines us to be more God like and free from all the sin, dysfunctions, and strongholds that the flesh, the world and the devil has brought upon us.

The Word, like a fire in us, does not just happen by chance or by God forcing it upon us. We have to desire it and even force ourselves at times to get it in us. What creates the desire for God's Word is to taste it and see that God is good. Then eat it and experience the joy and cleansing that comes as the result thereof.

Hebrews 4:12 reveals to us that God's Word is powerful and sharper than any two-edged sword and is a discerner of the thoughts and intents of our hearts. We all need attitude checks from time to time, and the best way to get the checkup is from the neck up. So the more we renew our minds with the Word of God the more our souls experience the transforming power of God. As Paul reveals in 2 Corinthians 4:16, our inward man can be renewed day by day.

Now Jeremiah 23:9 also talks about God's Word being a hammer that breaks rocks in pieces. Those rocks are our wrong attitudes and motives, areas of our life under Satan's control instead of God's control. So the more we let His Word in us the more it will break up the hard places in our hearts and lives. That is why James 1:21 (NIV) says, "Therefore, get rid of all moral filth and the evil that is so prevalent and humbly accept the Word planted in you, which can save you."

If you know that you are bound in all kind of lustful affections and desires, and your life is a wreck with no direction, joy or meaning, then open that Bible and begin reading. Ask God the Holy Spirit to speak to you and give you understanding, direction and application. You will be amazed at the things that will fall off you the more you read and study God's Word. Remember Jesus is the Word (John 1:1 and John 1:14). So the more Word you get in you, the more Jesus you get in you.

Jesus will heal your broken heart and set you free. But, how desperate are you? Are you desperate enough to spend quality and quantity time with Him? Pray this prayer: "God may your Word like a fire burn in me and burn things out of me, and may your Word like a hammer break up into pieces every area of hardness in my life, in Jesus' name".

Amen!!!

Humility And Tears

Acts 20:19

When you read Paul's letters to the Corinthians, you see that he is a no nonsense believer. He would rebuke and correct with Apostolic authority as the Spirit led him to do. There was another side to Paul though, and that was his humility and tears, as we see in Acts 20:19. Who else does that remind you of? Jesus, of course. He would rebuke the Pharisees, and speak tenderly to the hurting. Matthew 9:36 (NIV) records, "When he saw the crowds, he had compassion on them, because they were harassed and helpless, like sheep without a shepherd." Compassion is one of the Spirit-filled virtues in Colossians 3:12 with which, Paul said, we are to clothe ourselves. So the more we draw close to God the more our lives will reflect compassion and humility, even with tears.

I have always been one that had very sensitive eyes. They would water up very easily and I did not like that about myself. I would explain it away as a physical thing, but I think it is just the way God has wired me. So now I accept it as a gift from God. Tears are a reflection of compassion as our hearts reach out toward those who are hurting. The tears are an expression of intercession. Many times when I am ministering and praying over people, I begin to shed tears. I believe the Holy Spirit is shedding those tears through me as I pray.

Our hearts need to be moved to tears for all the pain and suffering people are going through in life. But tears alone do not change anything, but they can be the catalyst into Spirit-filled action.

It was the compassion of Jesus that led Him to teach, preach and heal. We see that in Matthew 9:35-36. In Romans 9:1-5, we see that Paul had great sorrow and anguish in his heart over the spiritual blindness of Israel. Even though Paul was called to minister to the Gentiles, he would always go to the Jews first and make every effort to convince them to believe in Jesus Christ as their savior. Listen to what the Spirit is saying through Paul in Galatians 4:19-20 (NIV), "My dear children, for whom I am again in the pains of childbirth until Christ is formed in you, how I wish I could be with you now and change my tone, because I am perplexed about you!" Paul was deeply moved for the Galatian church because false teachers were misleading them and he desired for them to grow up into Christ-like maturity. With this heart felt compassion he was led to write his letter to them.

As we see in Paul's life and ministry, even though God gives us power and authority, we are to always walk humbly before God and man. True humility will release God's power to flow more effectively into and through our lives. So we want to make sure that we never become proud of what God has done in us and through us.

Humility helps us to truly find our identity in Jesus Christ, because without Him I can do nothing (John 15:5). But through Him I can do all things, Philippians 4:13.

Amen!!!

What Are You A Slave To?

Romans 6:16 (NIV) "Don't you know that when you offer yourselves to someone to obey him as slaves, you are slaves to the one whom you obey—whether you are slaves to sin, which leads to death, or in obedience, which leads to righteousness?"

Who or what are you obeying today? Are you obeying the ways of the world, the council of the ungodly or the path of sinners? Are you sitting in the seat of the scornful? Or are you serving Jesus Christ wholeheartedly? Matthew 4:10 (NIV) records "Jesus said to him, 'Away from me Satan! For it is written: Worship the Lord your God, and serve Him only.'"

Our worship to God is not to be divided into a percentage of our attention. But it is to be all out, just as Jesus gave His all for us. If you are struggling with these questions and comments, then I suggest going to your knees and pray. Ask God to fill you with the power of His Spirit. It is only by the Spirit that we can worship and serve God wholeheartedly. Read Romans 8:12-17; these scriptures reveal that the Holy Spirit sets us free from sin, and leads us as sons of God to be worshipers, crying "Abba, Father".

Anything that takes all our time, energy, and money, and robs us of our relationship with God, is some kind of an idol in our lives. It could be too much work and the pursuit to be rich. It could be any form of exercise or hobby. Of course drugs and alcohol, and ungodly sexual relationships are idols too. Even wanting to please everyone all the time, or a compulsion to find happiness through your family. No person, thing or activity can take the place of God! But that is exactly where many people are, looking for happiness in all the wrong places. Even people in church get stuck in these lies and deceptions.

We were created with emptiness because of sin and only God can fill that void. But here again we need to let

God in completely. Let Him into those areas of pain, where you were abused and rejected. Only He can heal the brokenhearted. We cannot heal a wound by saying it is not there, or by placing a band-aid on it.

A common phrase today is "Let go and let God." What that means is I have to let go of trying to control my life and let God control every aspect of my life. The more we actually do so, the more we will actually experience God in a real and authentic way with healing and power. Jesus Christ died and rose from the grave in order to give us eternal life, that means having the very life of God abiding in us. His life in you has the capacity to set you free from the yokes and burdens in life that try to destroy you.

Will you yield to His life? It is a free gift to you; it cost Jesus a painful scourging and death on a cross. He gave His utmost for our highest; will you give your utmost for His highest? May you and I have the same attitude as Paul the Apostle when he said in 1 Corinthians 6:12b (NIV), "Everything is permissible for me – but I will not be mastered by anything." That takes us back to the main text, will you be a slave to sin or a slave to righteousness? I pray that you choose the latter!

Amen!!!

→ Read 1 Cor 6:12b

In Spite Of Strong Opposition

1 Thessalonians 2:1-6 (NIV) "You know, brothers, that our visit to you was not a failure. We had previously suffered and been insulted in Philippi as you know, but with the help of our God we dared to tell you His gospel in spite of strong opposition."

In Philippi, Paul and his companions had been insulted, beatened and imprisoned for preaching the Gospel. Now in Thessalonica more persecution and opposition was breaking out against them. God gave Paul and his team an uncommon boldness to keep preaching in spite of the opposition. There are several reasons why they had this uncommon boldness.

First, according to 1 Thessalonians 2:4, they spoke as men approved by God to be entrusted with the Gospel. They were not trying to please men but God, who tests our hearts. When you know that God has called you, sent you, and given you a specific vision then you will press on in Jesus' name no matter what comes against you. They had God's seal of approval bearing witness in their hearts. That is an awesome place to be, in God. That seal of approval comes through the revelation knowledge of God's great love for you and for the entire world.

When you are trying to get the approval of men, you can be easily persuaded to do certain things. Trying to have man's approval will cause many to water down the Gospel. Also, when you are serving under man's approval the Holy Spirit is not free to lead and do, as He wants. When that happens we begin to have religion instead of power. Ministering under man's approval will result in seeing fewer conversions, less healings and lives being set free. That is one of the reasons very few churches in America are seeing healings and miracles, and even salvations. Not that healings and miracles are to be our total emphasis, but they will come as a result of the Holy Spirit being completely free to minister as He wants. Just as Mark 16:20 (KJV) says, "And they went forth, and preached every where, the Lord working with them, and confirming the Word with signs following. Amen."

Secondly, they had this uncommon boldness in spite of opposition because they were not using flattery or masks to cover up greed. They preached the Gospel with pure motives. Their motive was for souls to be saved and completely changed in God. There were not any secret agendas, but to speak the truth of God's Word and nothing but the truth. Many times that comes with a price. The price of rejection and isolation, but it is always better to have only God's approval than the approval of a crowd. Paul taught the truth in some of his letters on how to prosper financially, but it was never for his personal gain. In looking at Paul's example, we preachers need to always examine our motives when talking about money.

Lastly, they had this uncommon boldness as a result of the gift of faith. 1 Corinthians 12:9 lists faith as one of the spiritual gifts. The gift of faith is different than saving faith or growing faith. The gift of faith is a supernatural endowment from the Holy Spirit to believe with great action in spite of the difficulties that may come against you. When the Holy Spirit tells you to go somewhere and speak and that Word is alive within you, you will go in spite of the opposition. There was a great boldness on Paul and his companions to persevere and that can only come from the Holy Spirit.

Paul and his team were daring in the face of danger. They always faced rejection and isolation. They always faced severe beatings and imprisonment. And ultimately they faced death, which finally came to Paul as a result of being an ambassador for the King of kings, Lord Jesus. Paul was beheaded for the Gospel, but he lived his life to the fullest according to God's divine purposes and calling.

Are you living your life to the fullest? Are you yielding to God's plan in spite of strong opposition? Or, are you giving in to the crowds and letting fear and man's approvals rule your life?

I pray that the Holy Spirit gives you revelation of His call and purpose for you and that you will respond with an over whelming, "Yes Lord, here am I. Send me!"

Amen!!!

My Joy Knows No Bounds

2 Corinthians 7:4b

Happiness comes from our emotions and positive circumstances in life but joy is an inner rejoicing in our spirit. "The kingdom of God is righteousness, peace and joy in the Holy Spirit." (Romans 14:17b NIV). Paul said in 2 Corinthians 7:4 (NIV) "In all my troubles my joy knows no bounds." Paul was able to rejoice in the Lord regardless of the difficulties in his life. Why was that so? Because the Gospel was being preached, lives were being changed and set free. Paul knew his purpose and mission in life and it was being fulfilled regardless of what the enemy brought against him. Paul knew the truth of Nehemiah 8:10 (KJV) that said, "...The joy of the Lord is your strength."

Not only is joy an inner rejoicing and strength, but also it is a weapon of our warfare. Look at Acts 16:16-34: Paul and Silas were stripped, beaten, severely flogged, thrown in prison, and shackled. At midnight they were praying and singing songs. As the result of their joy, God shook open the prison doors and broke free their shackles. They were able to stop the prison guard from killing himself and the guard and all his family got saved. More joy in our lives and churches will result in release from types of prisons and shackles that we are attached to. The joy abides within us in the Holy Spirit. We have to yield to that joy everyday and in every circumstance. It is like putting on a coat; the coat does not put itself on you, you abiding in God and God abiding in you.

Isaiah 61:1-3 tells us about joy that comes from God. The joy abounds because good news is preached, the brokenhearted are healed, and there's freedom for the captives bound in darkness. God gives favor and provides for the grieving. He gives us a crown of beauty instead of ashes, an oil of gladness instead of mourning and the garment of praise instead of despair.

Notice in 2 Corinthians 7:4 that the verse says, "My joy knows no bounds." The joy is the Holy Spirit in us and the Holy Spirit does not know boundaries and limitations. The Holy Spirit only knows the exceedingly, abundantly, immeasurably, limitless possibilities that we have in God. All things are possible with God and nothing is impossible for those that believe (Luke 1:37; Mark 9:23). Therefore we can choose joy instead of despair because great is our King and great are His promises.

In Luke 10:21, we see that Jesus was full of joy because the Father's work was being fulfilled on earth. We also see in Hebrew 12:2 that Jesus endured the cross because of the joy that was set before Him. My friend we are that joy, the souls that have come to Him as a result of His obedience. In John 17:13, Jesus prayed that we might have the full measure of His joy in us. We see that this prayer is fulfilled in our salvation as Peter said in 1 Peter 1:8, that we are filled with an inexpressible and glorious joy.

Zephaniah 3:17 (NIV), "The Lord your God is with you, He is mighty to save. He will take great delight in you, He will quiet you with His love, He will rejoice over you with singing." God is with us, in us, for us, delights in us, and rejoices over us. All the more reason for us to rejoice and be full of the joy of the Lord!

I pray that you choose joy and yield to joy for we have a great and awesome salvation!

Amen!!!

Jesus Came To Destroy The Works Of The Devil

1 John 3:8b (AMP) "The reason the Son of God was made manifest (visible) was to undo (destroy, loosen, and dissolve) the works the devil (has done)."

What works has the devil done? He rebelled and sinned against God. He tempts man to sin and leads man into a life of rebellion. He deceives and lies. Jesus called him the father of lies (John 8:44). He masquerades as an angel of light in order to deceive many with half-truths (2 Corinthians 11:13-15). The devil oppresses, rules and dominates people (Acts 10:38). He seduces people into destructive life styles. He attacks with sickness and disease (Luke 13:16; Mark 9:25-26). He is the accuser of the brethren (Revelation 12:10). He comes to steal, kill and destroy, (John 10:10). And like a roaring lion, he seeks whom he may devour (1 Peter 5:8). Jesus came to destroy the devil's work, or we could say, nullify and render inoperative.

Colossians 2:15, (NIV) "And having disarmed the powers and authorities, He made a public spectacle of them, triumphing over them by the cross." The first thing Jesus did to destroy the devil's work or render it inoperative was to die on the cross, shedding His blood in order to bring forgiveness and cleansing to the world. Once we receive Jesus' finished work on the cross as being enough for our sins to be forgiven, that begins the process of rendering Satan powerless in our lives (Ephesians 2:1-10). Revelation 12:11 (NKJV), "And they overcame him by the blood of the Lamb and by the word of their testimony." We need to see and understand by the Holy Spirit that Satan no longer has authority in our lives because Jesus shed His blood for us. We need to continually testify to this truth.

According to Hebrew 2:14-15, Jesus' resurrection has also rendered Satan powerless. Because of the resurrection, we no longer have to fear death and now Satan cannot render us as inoperative through fear of death. Also, the resurrection gives us a living hope (1 Peter 1:4). With living hope abiding in us we know that God is always with us and for us. Through this hope we find comfort, strength, and encouragement to keep believing and pressing onward and upward in Jesus' name. We also have His resurrection power abiding in us (Romans 8:11). And if the Holy Spirit can raise Jesus from the grave, He can raise us up and over any kind of demonic attacks. 1 John 4:4 (NKJV), "He who is in you is greater than he who is in the world."

1 Peter 5:9 tells us to resist the devil, standing firm in the faith. Our faith rests in Jesus dying on the cross and in His bodily resurrection. This is the Gospel of Jesus Christ and in this simple truth Satan is rendered powerless in our lives, if we stand on the truth. There is authority in the name of Jesus to resist the devil (Luke10:17-19; Mark 16:17).

Lastly, we are reminded in Ephesians 4:25-32 not to give the devil a foothold into our lives. A foothold is an open door into our lives whereby we give Satan authority to attack and even defeat us. That foothold can come by way of a continued sin, doubt, unbelief, fear, and by the words we speak. We also open the door by our lack of knowledge (Hosea 4:6). So I pray that this exhortation gives you some knowledge that the victorious life is yours to walk out and receive.

May God open the eyes of your heart to realize the power and authority that you have in Jesus' name and that Jesus has already rendered the devil powerless and ineffective in your life. Stand firm in these truths and never give into fear. Fight the good fight of faith!

Amen!!!

Take Heed What You Hear

Mark 4:24-25 (NKJV) Then He said to them, "Take heed what you hear. With the same measure you use, it will be measured to you; and to you who hear, more will be given. For whoever has, to him more will be given; but whoever does not have, even what he has will be taken away from him."

To take heed means to pay close attention or to listen carefully. What kind of attention are you giving towards what you hear? There is much difference between hearing and listening. Many times we hear the noise all around us and even hear the words someone is speaking. But listening is all about paying close attention, whether you are listening to people or to God.

When we take heed to what we hear, we are careful not to listen to negative, worldly, or demonic voices. What we listen to on the radio or television has a big impact on our lives. All those wrong voices have the power to pull us down, if we allow them to. So it is important that we protect ourselves from all the trash on the airwaves.

We need to make sure we are not listening to demonic voices from the past that are saying, "You are worthless, you're a nobody, you won't amount to anything." or the voices that accuse and condemn from sins in our past. Evil spirits will always try to whisper thoughts into our minds as a way to oppress and weaken us, trying to destroy our testimonies. That is why 2 Corinthians 10:3-6 (NKJV) says, "For though we walk in the flesh, we do not war according to the flesh. For the weapons of our warfare are not carnal but mighty in God for pulling down strongholds, casting down arguments and every high thing that exalts itself against the knowledge of God, bringing every thought into captivity to the obedience of Christ." These spirits will bring arguments and false claims against the knowledge of Christ. If we are not taking heed to what we are hearing those pretentious thoughts can bring us into bondage, which is what the Bible calls spiritual strongholds.

Sometimes what we hear will cause fear and doubt. That is why it is important that we consistently read, study, meditate, memorize and hear God's Word. Our discipline in the Word of God will impart faith and confidence. Ephesians 6:16 (NKJV) says, "Above all, taking the shield of faith with which you will be able to quench all the fiery darts of the wicked one." The shield of faith is God's Word and the fiery darts are those demonic thoughts and voices.

The measure of our hearing is all about how careful we are to listen to God and not to the wrong voices. Are you getting alone with God? Are you reserving a quiet time isolated from outside noise and distractions? Are you applying yourself to hear? Try worshiping with soft music, reading and listening to the Bible and just being still and listening. God will speak and He has been speaking. Remember, prayer is not just you speaking but it is God speaking too. It is to be a dialogue not monologue.

Mark 4:24 (NKJV) says, "And to you who hear, more will be given." God will speak more and direct you more; the more you apply yourself to listen. But if we go through life fast, hearing all the noise and the wrong voices we will hear God less and less.

When Jesus said in verse 25, "But whoever does not have, even what he has will be taken away from him." Jesus is talking about whoever does not have ears to hear. And as a result of not applying ourselves to hear, what we have heard in the past will be taken away. The taking away is the enemy taking from us because we are not taking heed to our hearing. The taking away can also be losing faith and having doubt. It could be losing our health or a healing, or financial blessings. It could even be losing joy and peace. This is all the result of the measure of our hearing.

Lastly, I encourage you to listen to the words and dreams that come through the night. As our bodies sleep, our spirit is always alert, and the Holy Spirit will speak in the night. So pay attention and take heed; God has many things

to say to you and through you. He has great things in store for your life. Do not miss out because you are not listening!
Amen!!!

I Pursued My Enemy

Psalm 18:37-40 (NKJV) "I have pursued my enemies and overtaken them; neither did I turn back again till they were destroyed. I have wounded them, so that they could not rise; they have fallen under my feet. For you have armed me with strength for the battle; You have subdued under me those who rose up against me. You have also given me the necks of my enemies, so that I destroyed those who hated me."

This is a Psalm of David. These are the words David spoke to God who delivered him from his enemies. In reading this Psalm we see that God works with us, in us and through us when He delivers us from our enemies. We are to cooperate with God and follow His leading when we cry out for help.

Notice in Psalm 18:1-2 David expresses his love towards God. Then he confesses that God is his rock, fortress, deliverer, and strength in which he trusts. In any battles that you go through in life, it is important to get God on your side by expressing your love to Him and acknowledging the blessings you have with Him and in Him. The more you tell God that you trust Him the more it reinforces to you that God is with you. This will also help push away fear. In Psalm 18:3 (NKJV) David expresses his praise towards God, and then says, "So shall I be saved from my enemies." Our praise helps to bring our deliverance and protection that God provides. Psalm 22:3 (NKJV) says, "But you are holy, enthroned in the praises of Israel." God inhabits our praise, thus causing His presence to be more tangible to us, bringing forth our protection. I love Psalm 32:7 (NKJV), "You are my hiding place; You shall preserve me from trouble; You shall surround me with songs of deliverance." It is in that hiding place of abiding in Christ and Christ abiding in us that we find protection. The Holy Spirit gives us those songs of deliverance. As we sing in and by the Spirit, God surrounds us with protection. So we see that there are some foundational aspects of our faith relationship with God that brings us to the place of being able to pursue our enemies.

Now the real enemy is the devil himself and all his demons. As Paul said in Ephesians 6:12 (NKJV), "For we do not wrestle against flesh and blood, but against principalities, against powers, against the rulers of the darkness of this age, against spiritual hosts of wickedness in the heavenly places." Even when you think a person is your enemy, remember there may be evil spirits behind all the hate, selfishness, lies and deception, and division that is being manifested. James 3:14-16 makes that very clear.

All of us as born-again believers in Jesus Christ should be in hot pursuit of our real enemy. I am not talking about flesh and blood enemies but the prince of the power of the air (Ephesians 2:2). The way we pursue Him is not by doing some kind of witch-hunt, but by doing the will of the Father. Light will always expose darkness and dispel it. So as we walk in the light as He is in the light, we will be pursuing our real enemy. As Jesus said in Matthew 16:18 (NKJV), "And on this rock I will build My church, and the gates of Hades will not prevail against it." The gates of hell will not prevail against us, not because we have a good defensive strategy, but because we have an offensive strategy of hot pursuit. Jesus continued saying in Matthew 16:19 (NKJV), "And I will give you the keys of the kingdom of heaven, and whatever you bind on earth will be bound in heaven, and whatever you loose on earth will be loosed in heaven." The keys of the kingdom are His power and authority given to us by grace. These Words are a call to action!

Going back to Psalm 18:37, David pursued his enemies, overtook them, and did not turn back till they were destroyed. What enemies do you need to pursue and overtake? Are there any addictive actions in your life? Do you struggle with any form of co-dependency? Are there any health or financial issues that you need to overtake? David

56

ran towards Goliath when he was taunted. Do not give in to the enemy's schemes and tactics, but run towards him with boldness and confidence.

As you continue to walk in the Spirit, rejoicing in your salvation and doing the Father's will, you will see deliverance and protection, and mighty breakthroughs in your life!

Amen!!!

Like A Flood The Spirit Of The Lord Will Lift Up A Standard

Isaiah 59:19b (NKJV) "When the enemy comes in like a flood, the Spirit of the Lord will lift up a standard against him."

In the original Hebrew text there was not a comma after the word flood. Man inserted the comma. With the comma after the word flood it sounds like the enemy gets credit for turbulent flood like attacks.

We all know that sometimes the devil's attacks feel like we have been hit blind-sided. But I would rather not give the devil too much credit. I personally stick to the thought of giving God credit for the flood like power that comes against the devil. So whatever Satan says or does to us, like a flood the Spirit of the Lord will lift up a standard against him! Think of it as the floodgates of heaven being released against our enemy.

The devil is no match for the Spirit of the living God. Remember the Holy Spirit lives and abides within you, so the devil is no match for you or I either. Just as Isaiah 10:27 mentions the yoke destroying and burden removing power of God. The yokes and burdens are in reference to Satan's oppressive attacks, but the anointing, which is the Holy Spirit, will bring victory into our lives as we yield to Him.

Focus on all the grace that God gives in opposition to what the devil gives: Love versus hate. Forgiveness versus rejection. Eternal life versus eternal damnation. Resurrection power versus death. The oil of gladness versus mourning. A garment of praise versus despair. A crown of beauty versus ashes, freedom versus captivity. Peace versus worry. Faith versus doubt. Courage versus fear. Healing versus sickness. Provision and prosperity versus poverty. These are just some of the blessings that we have in comparison to what the devil gives.

2 Peter 1:3 (NIV) says, "His divine power has given us

everything we need for life and godliness through our knowledge of Him." "Knowledge of Him" is in reference to Jesus. As we grow through our knowledge of what Jesus has provided and accomplished for us through the cross and resurrection; the Holy Spirit will then manifest it into our lives. So whatever Satan brings against you do not sweat it; God has a standard from His Word to retaliate.

Always pray and listen to what the Holy Spirit will say in any situation in life. This is exactly what James was talking about in James 1:5 when God gives us wisdom in the midst of our trials. Always be aware of the presence of the Holy Spirit, get to know Him and talk to Him. As you do you will experience flood-like power in your life. Jesus said in John 7:37-38 that out of our inner most being will flow rivers of living water. Well, that living water is the Holy Spirit flowing from the floodgates of heaven. Psalm 46:4 also makes mention of this.

So I encourage you to get under the spout where the glory comes out. Let your prayer be, "Open the floodgates of heaven and let it rain!" God will be glorified, you will over-come, and the devil will be defeated, every time, no matter what comes your way!

Amen!!!

Where Sin Abounded, Grace Abounded Much More (1)

Romans 5:20b (NKJV)

The end result of sin is death and judgment. The end result of grace is life and justification. In John 10:10b (NKJV), Jesus said, "I have come that they might have life, and that they may have it more abundantly." We know that sin is rebellion and disobedience towards God, but what is grace? Simply put grace is God's riches for you at Christ's expense. Grace is God's favor paid for by Jesus dying on the cross. What kind of favor, you may ask? Anything and everything according to our present need. But of course our biggest need is to have God in our lives, filling that empty void that was created by sin.

In speaking of where sin abounded, we must first look at the sin of rejecting God as our Lord and savior, as opposed to any specific sins. That sin of rebellion has man on a fast track straight to hell. But when grace interjects, hell is bypassed and man is now heaven bound. No longer do we have to face death with fear. As 1 John 4:17 reminds us, love has been perfected in us that we can have boldness in the day of judgment.

"Where sin abounded" speaks of a place or a time and season when sin was on the increase in our lives. It could have been years ago, yesterday or 5 minutes ago. There is a spiritual law found in Galatians 6:7-8 (NKJV), "Do not be deceived, God is not mocked; for whatever a man sows, that he will also reap. For he who sows to the flesh will of the flesh reap corruption, but he who sows to the Spirit will of the Spirit reap everlasting life."

Abounding sin deals with the condition of our heart. The more we yield to sin, the harder our heart becomes. We will become dull of hearing and spiritually blind. Drinking too much alcohol can abound to anger issues, brawling, domestic violence, auto accidents and being imprisoned.

Unchecked looks at the opposite sex can turn into lust, pornography, adultery, broken marriages and broken homes. These are just a few examples of the results of abounding sin.

Now grace does not abound in the midst of a continued life of sin but it abounds when there is repentance from that sin. The good news is that God does not require us to straighten up our life. He simply says, "Come to Him and He will do the changing within you." That is grace! Where sin caused all kinds of destruction in someone's life, grace can turn things around. You still might have to face some of the consequences of wrong choices, but grace can bring restoration and hope into a very hopeless situation. Even though sin has an abounding force in life, grace has a much more abounding force. In other words, grace will bring increase where sin had brought decrease and destruction.

"For if by one man's offense death reigned through the one, much more those who receive abundance of grace and of the gift of righteousness will reign in life through the One, Jesus Christ." (Romans 5:17 NKJV). To receive the abundance of grace is all about us yielding to the power of the Holy Spirit daily and not trying to add to His grace. Simply believe and receive His love and favor in a growing relationship with Him.

To reign in life through Jesus means we will reign like a king over the power of sin. We do not have to yield to sin. The power of God's grace in His Spirit will give us victory over any and all temptations. The choice is yours—death or life, sin or grace, victory or defeat! As for me, I choose to reign in life by my Lord Jesus and submit to His abounding grace! What about you? What choice will you make today?

Amen!!!

Where Sin Abounded, Grace Abounded Much More (2)

Romans 5:20b (NKJV)

The law of gravity is real whether you believe so or not. Just jump off a building and test the theory.

The same is true with sin. When sin is on the increase in your life, it will bring destruction and hardness of heart. But the law of grace is also true. When you yield to Jesus, who is all encompassing of grace, grace will bring increase of favor and blessings. Grace is all of God's love, goodness, favor and power poured out into our lives by the Holy Spirit as God's gift to us because Jesus paid it all. Just as the law of aerodynamics will over-power the law of gravity, so will grace over-power the effects of sin.

So where sin has brought confusion and lack of direction, grace will bring clarity and wisdom. Where sin has brought depression, discouragement, and despair, grace will bring joy and laughter and hope. Where sin has split a family apart, grace can restore a family. Where sin has brought poverty and sickness, grace will bring provision and healing. Where sin has brought us into doubt and fear, grace will bring faith and fearlessness.

Some may say, "But I don't deserve these blessings. I'm so unworthy." That is absolutely true. It is God's goodness and kindness that lead us to repentance (Romans 2:4). Or someone may think they have to clean up their lives first before coming to God or experiencing His love. Saying, "Thank you, God. Have mercy on me." is a good place to start. The good news of grace is that we do not earn God's favor and we do not have to strive at being good enough. We receive it by faith with thanksgiving.

When we fall as Christians (and we all do), God does not condemn us (Romans 8:1). We want to be careful that sin does not harden our hearts, so therefore we do confess it. God does not close the door to us because we have committed certain sins or because of how many times we have sinned in a day. We want to make sure that we do not miss God's will and calling on our lives because we are condemning ourselves. Nothing can separate us from the love of God in Christ Jesus (Romans 8:39). "For God's gifts and His call are irrevocable." (Romans 11:29 NIV).

The joy of our salvation overflows in us because His grace is so awesome and wonderful. Where we tend to lose our joy is when we think we have to earn everything. Yes, God rewards diligent faith, according to Hebrews 11:6. But our faith is in His grace. They flow together, like a hand in glove.

So I encourage you to enter into the joy of your salvation. Let His grace abound in you. Believe it and receive it. Stop trying to earn it. Trust in the hope that grace brings. God wants you and I to walk in His power, favor, love and blessings. What choice will you make?

"As for me and my house we will serve the Lord." (Joshua 24:15 NKJV).

Amen!!!

Restoring Grace

Galatians 6:1-2 (NIV) "Brothers, if someone is caught in a sin, you who are spiritual should restore him gently. But watch yourself, or you also may be tempted. Carry each other's burdens, and in this way you will fulfill the law of Christ."

This Word of instruction does not mean that you are called to look for sin in someone's life. "If someone is caught in a sin..." More than anything, this phrase is speaking of a person that has been overtaken by a particular sin. When a person has become weak and keeps falling in the same area, gentleness, humility and love are the necessary tools to help restore such a person.

Even though Jesus said in Matthew 12:33b (NIV), "A tree is recognized by its fruit", we are not to judge one another. Not judging someone does not mean you cannot acknowledge what you see in someone, nor does it mean that you cannot confront someone of his or her sin. But we are not to self-righteously accuse and condemn. We should always look at our own lives with humility, "but by the grace of God, there go I". Pride always comes before the fall. It is when we think we are above falling that we become the most vulnerable.

To be overtaken by a sin could be a learned behavior in the environment in which someone grew up. They may have learned sin from parents, siblings or the culture. It could be a generational sin that has been passed down from generation to generation. It could also be a sin of coping to an evil environment of abuse. It could also be a sin that a person cherishes.

The spiritual person that restores such a person is one that is walking in the Spirit. The spiritual person is full of the fruit of the Spirit (Galatians 5:22-23). The spiritual person will also operate in the gifts of the Spirit (1 Corinthians 12:7-11 and Romans 12:6-8). The spiritual person that helps bring restoration is to do so with gentleness. God will love them through you. If you do not have compassion for the hurting person, then you are not the one to help restore them. But the Holy Spirit will fill you with compassion as you pray for people.

Gentleness is also known as meekness. Meekness is a mixture of humility, boldness and confidence. When ministering restoration, we need to humbly and gently speak to people and at times boldly declare God's Word to them.

Galatians 6:2 says, "Carry each other's burdens, and in this way you will fulfill the law of Christ." This is in reference to the type of burdens that has a person weighed down with pressure—the type of pressure that is called yokes and spiritual strongholds, where there is demonic oppression. Someone that is trained in dealing with these kind of burdens is necessary. Also, having a working and relational knowledge of the grace of Jesus Christ. This is the same knowledge of grace that Romans 5:17 and 20 talk about.

In surveying all of this truth for ministering restoration we see that the law of Christ is fulfilled. The law of Christ is loving God and loving your neighbor just like Jesus proclaimed in Mark 12:29-31. As we seek to love and honor God in our lives there will always be people that we cross paths with that could use our help to bring restoration to them.

I pray that you will be sensitive to the Holy Spirit's leading and prompting. Many times it might be a team of people in the body of Christ to help bring restoration. Some will pray, some will give love, others will minister the Word of God, and some will flow in special gifts that are needed to bring healing and deliverance. What role will you play in giving hope to the weary soul? The prerequisite is that you are spiritual, full of the Spirit.

So, my brothers and sisters, it is time to step up to the plate, and get on base. Make your life count for someone!
Amen!!!

The Lord Is Close To The Brokenhearted

Psalm 34:18 (NIV) "The Lord is close to the brokenhearted and saves those who are crushed in spirit."

The reality is that every person alive who does not have God in his or her life is brokenhearted. There are different degrees of brokenness. Many will fill their lives with other things and cover up their pain, but underneath it all there is brokenness. Only God can heal a broken heart. He is the chief surgeon. What appears to be impossible to man is always possible with God. Too often man's remedy is to prescribe medication. But usually that only masks the pain, it does not heal.

It is exciting to see the Master's touch when one is completely crushed. I was ministering at a Christian Men's retreat years ago and the Holy Spirit called for an unplanned anointing service in the chapel. One man that came forward had a very dark cloud of despair all over him. We found out that his son had committed suicide, his wife had left him, he lost his job, and he was suicidal himself. He did not even want to be at this retreat. It was a miracle of divine appointment. When he came forward for prayer, as hands were laid on him, he literally felt the fire of God go through his heart. Instantly his broken heart was healed and all the darkness left him. For the rest of the weekend, he was full of joy and he began to follow God. I have been a part of God's divine healings many times. He is awesome!

Such healings happen because God is close to the brokenhearted and saves those that are crushed in spirit. The devil is always looking to destroy lives and God is always looking to restore lives. Sometimes the healing is instant and miraculous as I shared in the testimony. Other times it is a continual process. Whether it is instant or gradual, the remedies are: getting God's Word into you, a lifestyle of prayer and praise, and letting godly people get close to you. We all need godly friends, friends that will minister healing, praying with us and for us. Also, friends that will sharpen us and challenge us.

One of the biggest obstacles to healing a broken heart is letting God and people get close enough to you. Many times painful memories get locked away and ignored, but in so doing this disease festers out into our lives and relationships. Yes, it is painful to face and deal with certain issues. But as we do, we pass through the threshold of healing.

In Psalm 147:2-4 we read that God builds up Jerusalem, heals the brokenhearted, determines the number of stars and calls them by name. Many times in ignorance, people will say things like, "God has too many big and important things to do than to concern Himself with me." This Psalm is a good one to refute that line of thinking. Here God is building a nation and naming the stars, and in between He takes time to heal a broken heart. Not to mention the fact that building a nation is all about broken people being restored.

When God binds a wound, He does not just put a band-aid on it. He pours in the healing oil. The healing oil is His Holy Spirit. That is why we, as ministers of God, need to be full of the Spirit and sensitive to His leading. Psalm 147:5 (NIV) reads, "Great is our Lord and mighty in power; His understanding has no limit." There are not any hearts that His power cannot heal and He understands every tiny detail of what hurts. There are not any problems that are beyond His comprehension.

So, I encourage everyone to look up for He is the lifter of the head. There is hope for the hopeless and there is power to redeem. Let God anoint you with the oil of gladness and deliver you from the memories of ashes and despair.

God is real. He is awesome and powerful, full of goodness and mercy. Nothing is impossible with Him!

Amen!!!

The Strongholds That Become The Accepted Norm

1 Samuel Chapters 18-20 (NIV)

1 Samuel 18:6-7 (NIV) reads: "When the men were returning home after David had killed the Philistine, the women came out from all the towns of Israel to meet King Saul with singing and dancing, with joyful songs and with tambourines and lutes. As they danced, they sang: "Saul has slain his thousands, and David his tens of thousands." Verses 8-9 declare that Saul was very angry and jealous of David, and verse 15 says he was afraid of David. Verses 10-11 declare that an evil spirit forcefully came upon Saul and he tried to kill David.

The anger, jealousy and fear of Saul were his choices. These wrong choices gave the devil an open door to forcefully come upon Saul. At that point, the anger, jealousy and fear became spiritual strongholds; whereby Saul was obsessed and oppressed.

1 Samuel 19:1 reads, "Saul told his son Jonathan and all the attendants to kill David." Now Saul was obsessed with killing David. Instead of running the affairs of the nation as their Commander in Chief, Saul was obsessively chasing David all over the countryside trying to kill David. This is how the enemy works: by getting our focus on ourselves and off of God, we will begin to obsess. In so doing we lose sight of our main call and the purpose for which we were created.

1 Samuel 19:18-24 is a perfect example of what Isaiah 59:19 teaches: when the enemy comes against us, like a flood the Spirit of the Lord will lift up a standard against him. What we see in 1 Samuel 19:18-24 is that Saul had sent three different groups of men to capture David who was with Samuel the prophet. When the groups of men got close to Samuel and his company of prophets that were prophesying, they too began to prophesy as the Spirit of God came upon them. Finally, Saul came looking for David and the Spirit of

God came upon him and he began to prophesy. Saul laid prostrate before God and Samuel in the presence of God.

It would be awesome if the story ended there, but once Saul left the presence of God with the company of prophets, he went back to what he was familiar with. We see in 1 Samuel 20:30-33 that Saul was once again obsessed with killing David, even to the point, that he was angry with his son Jonathan and hurled a spear at him.

In the Old Testament, the Holy Spirit would come and go. He would only rest upon people to do certain tasks. In the New Testament the Holy Spirit abides within us and we are sealed with Him. Therefore we have a much stronger capacity to overcome evil because the Spirit is always in us as born-again believers. However, we see a spiritual principle in this story. Just as Saul made wrong choices and yielded to sin, he opened the door to demonic oppression and obsession in his life. Christians can also open that same door with wrong choices. Also, even when we are experiencing a close walk in the Spirit, we can be enticed to go back to old familiar ways. I have personally seen people have mountaintop experiences with God on retreats, only to fall again into the valley.

It is important to take what we have received on the mountaintop and apply it to the valleys in life. Jesus said in Mark 4:16-17 (NIV), "Others, like seed sown on rocky places, hear the Word and at once receive it with joy. But since they have no root, they last only a short time. When trouble or persecution comes because of the Word, they quickly fall away."

So I encourage you to realize that sin is always knocking. Let the Word get deeply rooted in you and stay full of the Spirit everyday. You cannot take a vacation from being strong. The devil is always seeking whom he may devour. Do not open that door but instead devour him and his kingdom as you daily yield to the Holy Spirit!

Amen!!!

He Was Bruised For Our Iniquities

Isaiah 53:5 (NKJV) "But He was wounded for our transgressions, He was bruised for our iniquities."

Jesus was wounded on the outside of His body to bring cleansing for our outward transgressions of breaking God's laws. Jesus was bruised, which is an injury to body tissue without breaking the skin. So Jesus was bruised inwardly to bring cleansing to us for iniquities, which is our inward sins. Matthew 15:18-19 (NKJV) reads, "But those things which proceed out of the mouth come from the heart, and they defile a man. For out of the heart proceed evil thoughts, murders, adulteries, fornications, thefts, false witness, blasphemies." Jesus' death on the cross paid the debt for all our sins, both inward and outward.

Hosea 4:6 (NKJV) reads, "My people are destroyed for lack of knowledge." It is important to understand that Jesus was bruised for our iniquities, because many Christians still struggle with inward sins. Sin is like a shackle that binds us. The cleansing power of the blood of Jesus will break the shackles of sin. The word "cleansing" can also mean, to be set free and liberated from the power of sin. Isaiah 1:18 (NKJV) gives us a clear picture of Jesus' cleansing blood. "Come now, and let us reason together." says the Lord. "Though your sins are like scarlet, they shall be as white as snow; though they are red like crimson, they shall be as wool." And 1 John 1:9 (NKJV) reads, "If we confess our sins, He is faithful and just to forgive us our sins and to cleanse us from all unrighteousness."

The day we called on Jesus to be our Savior and confessed Him as our Lord, the Holy Spirit took up residence in us making us new and alive, and, according to 2 Corinthians 5:17, we became a new creation, in our spirit. 1 Corinthians 6:17 reads, "But he who is joined to the Lord is one spirit with Him." Our spirit-man is forgiven once and for all, perfect and united with the Holy Spirit. But our heart is made up of two parts: spirit and soul. The soul is also inward, which is the mind, will and emotions. The soul-man is not perfect in Christ and has to be renewed daily. Confessing our sins that come from our inward soul and submitting them to the cleansing blood of Jesus will bring victory and freedom, spirit, soul and body.

If there are any iniquities that we struggle with, submitting them to Jesus' finished work of being bruised for us will bring victory. Also according to 2 Corinthians 4:16 and Romans 12:2, our souls will be transformed daily as we renew our minds to what God's Word says. And 2 Corinthians 3:17-18 reminds us that we will be transformed from glory to glory by the Spirit of the Lord. Here again what is in the process of transformation is our soul-man, because the spirit-man has already been made new in Christ.

So I encourage you to confess your sins when they are committed, inward and outward, not allowing hardness and strongholds to build up in your soul and body. Renew your mind daily with God's Word, and, according to Ephesians 3:16, may you be strengthened with power by God's Spirit in your inner being. The end result will be according to 1 Thessalonians 5:23 (NKJV), "Now may the God of peace Himself sanctify you completely; and may your whole spirit, soul, and body be preserved blameless at the coming of our Lord Jesus Christ."

Amen!!!

Walk In The Spirit, And You Shall Not Fulfill The Lust Of The Flesh

Galatians 5:16-17 (NKJV) "I say then: Walk in the Spirit, and you shall not fulfill the lust of the flesh. For the flesh lust against the Spirit, and the Spirit against the flesh; and these are contrary to one another."

Paul the Apostle continues his letter in Galatians 5:19-26 showing the contrast between the sins of the flesh and the fruit of the Spirit. Galatians 5:22-23 (NKJV) reads, "But the fruit of the Spirit is love, joy, peace, long-suffering, kindness, goodness, faithfulness, gentleness, self-control. Against such there is no law."

Now when the Bible talks about "the flesh" it is in reference to the evil desires in our fallen human nature. These evil desires are seen in the form of selfishness and sin, and anything that is contrary to God. Galatians 5:19-21 gives us a list of the sins of the flesh. This is not an exhausted list because at the end of verse 21 it reads "and the like". So there can be many other sins of the flesh that are similar to those listed.

To walk in the Spirit is to keep on walking through life depending on the indwelling Holy Spirit for power and guidance. We have to depend on the Holy Spirit, or else we will walk in the lust of the flesh. But when we go through life depending on the Holy Spirit, we will experience power and victory against any form of temptation.

So what does walking in the Spirit consist of? It will always consist of a vibrant prayer life, being in constant fellowship with the Spirit. Paul had also made reference to this in 2 Corinthians 13:14. In reading Paul's prayer for the church in Ephesians 3:16 (NKJV) we see the importance of depending on the Holy Spirit daily, "that He would grant you, according to the riches of His glory, to be strengthened with might through His Spirit in the inner man."

So in our prayers we literally express, "Holy Spirit, I depend on you today. I yield to your leading and providential appointments. I yield to your power and authority. I yield to the fruit of the Spirit and the gifts of the Spirit. I yield to you as my prayer partner and I yield to you in speaking to me through God's Word. Have your way with me, in me, and through me. I yield to seeing eyes, hearing ears, and a discerning heart. To God be the glory." In this type of a daily prayer, we are relinquishing all control to the Holy Spirit. When we live our lives under His control, then we will not get out of control. I also suggest praying prostrate on the floor or on your knees, as a way of expressing dependence with humility.

There is much to be said about the "Spirit-filled life". I believe this word of exhortation is a good place to start and to continue in. As you apply these truths to your life, as a new way of life, you will see a change in character, strength, and victory in your life!

Amen!!!

The Spirit Yearns For Our Fellowship

James 4:1-10 (NKJV)

James 4:5 (NKJV) "The Spirit who dwells in us yearns jealously."

James chapter 4 is written to the Church. He addresses the fact that there is fighting, lust, selfish desires, and friendship with the world. He calls this adultery against God. There is no fellowship with the Spirit when we are living this kind of lifestyle. But instead of rejecting us, the Spirit still yearns to have a close fellowship with us. I believe that is why James 4:6 says, "But He gives more grace."

Because the debt for our sin has already been paid by the death of Jesus, there is always grace for repentance, and grace for renewed fellowship with God. No matter how many times a day we may fall, His grace always forgives and restores. That gives us hope; for great is His love.

But it is important to understand that the Holy Spirit has feelings and according to Ephesians 4:30 the Holy Spirit can be grieved. He is grieved when we sin, especially when we continue to sin. He feels rejected and hurt as if we do not want any part of Him. That is why James called friendship with the world adultery against God. The ways of the world and the lustful desires become a mistress. So, just like a heartbroken wife waiting for her cheating husband to come home, the Holy Spirit also waits with intense yearning.

He waits with intense yearning because God loves us and the Holy Spirit is God. The Holy Spirit wants to talk to us, just like a husband and wife would talk to one another that are deeply in love. The Holy Spirit wants to lead us and comfort us through our trials in life. The Holy Spirit wants to teach us what has been freely given to us from God (1 Corinthians 2:12). He wants to change us into His image (Galatians 5:22-23). He also wants to empower us for His service (Acts 1:8). And He wants to be our prayer and worship partner (Romans 8:14-16, 26-27). There is much to learn and receive from the Holy Spirit, as we walk in fellowship with Him.

Now, as James 4:6-8 points out, we need to humble ourselves to enjoy this intimacy with the Holy Spirit. You may want to examine your heart to see if there are any prideful ways in you. Let God's Word and Spirit examine you. Along with that examination there needs to be submission to God in what He shows you. Out of the humility and submission, God draws close to you because you drew close to Him. Then and only then we have the power and authority to resist the devil. Otherwise we are just blowing in the wind, trying to get the devil out of our lives.

We also see in James 4:8-10 that there is a time to be heartbroken for our sins. Broken to the point of mourning, and once again purifying our hearts and repenting from being double-minded. The apostle John gives us a similar exhortation in 1 John chapter one. Also, James reminds us in chapter 1:6-8 that a double-minded man is unstable in all his ways, being tossed about, like the waves of the sea.

James 4:10 reads, "Humble yourselves in the sight of the Lord, and He will lift you up." James gives us this Word of admonition by the Holy Spirit because the Holy Spirit does yearn for intimacy with us. The end result is that when we have this intimacy with Him, our lives will be lifted up. We will be lifted up in victory over the flesh and the devil! We will be lifted up in victory over any obstacles in life! We will be lifted up in faith and confidence! And we will be lifted up in promotion! Therefore, we will shine as bright lights in the midst of a crooked and perverse generation (Philippians 2:15).

Amen!!!

Abundance Of Your House & River Of Delights

Psalm 36:8 (NIV) "They feast on the abundance of your house; You give them drink from Your river of delights."

This Psalm flows in imagery, similar to Psalm 63:5 (NIV), "My soul will be satisfied as with the riches of foods." And Psalm 42:1 (NIV), "As the deer pants for streams of water, so my soul pants for you, O God." Also Psalm 46:4 (NIV) reads, "There is a river whose streams make glad the city of God, the Holy place where the Most High dwells." What we see here are pictures of the presence of God, and wherever His presence is there is an abundant provision of His Spirit to fill and satisfy His people in an ever-consuming fashion.

Jesus said in Matthew 21:13 (NKJV), "My house shall be called a house of prayer." And Jesus said in Matthew 18:20 (NKJV), "For where two or three are gathered together in My name, I am there in the midst of them." Going back to Psalm 36:8, there is something special that takes place when God's people get together in His house of worship to pray. That house of worship could be any house that someone lives in, or the place we call church. Just as Psalm 93:5 (NKJV) says, "Holiness adorns Your house, O Lord, forever." We actually feast on His holiness, thus making us holy. God's presence will always affect us in a special way. With this being said, there is a corporate anointing that settles on God's people when we come together to seek His face. I know when we have prayer meetings at our church, I want to lay prostrate on the floor, not to be seen by man, but because it is holy and I want to humbly submit to His holiness.

Drinking from God's river of delights is a picture of drinking in the life of the Spirit in total consumption. 1 Corinthians 12:13b (NIV) reads, "And we were all given the one Spirit to drink." As we yield to the Holy Spirit in relationship, His leading, control and power, we are actually drinking. According to Psalm 23:5 as we drink, our cup will overflow. We will overflow with all the fruit of the Spirit, which is life changing, and attitude rearranging. We will also overflow with the gifts of the Spirit and special anointings. The more time we spend drinking in the life of the Spirit, the more pleasure and delight we will actually experience in our lives. God's pleasures and delights do not compare to the world's pleasures. When we drink from the Spirit we have joy and laughter in abundance without any hangovers. Praise God!

When our lives are totally committed to God, spending time with Him and yielding to Him, we will be feasting in abundance and drinking from the river of delights. Thus our souls will be very satisfied!

How about you? Will you feast on the abundance of His house and drink from the river of His delights?

Amen!!!

Given Over To Death For Jesus' Sake

2 Corinthians 4:7-12 (NKJV)

The Holy Spirit is leading me to write on this subject in contrast to the "River Of Delights." Even though the Spirit-filled life is a life of joy and blessings in abundance, as a surrendered Ambassador of Jesus Christ, you will go through many hardships for the sake of the Gospel. Just as Jesus suffered reproach and ultimately death, the call on many will consist of similar sufferings and reproach. But the good news is that God's grace will always be sufficient to sustain and empower us for what we may go through.

2 Corinthians 4:8-12 (NKJV) reads, "We are hard-pressed on every side, yet not crushed; we are perplexed, but not in despair; persecuted, but not forsaken; struck down, but not destroyed — always carrying about in the body the dying of the Lord Jesus, that the life of Jesus also may be manifested in our body. For we who live are always delivered to death for Jesus' sake, that the life of Jesus also may be manifested in our mortal flesh. So then death is working in us, but life in you." In these scriptures we see that in struggles, God is always with us. Even though a type of death is at work within us for Christ's sake, there is still the ongoing life of Jesus at work within us as well. Actually, the life that is manifested in us while death is at work in us is a testimony of God's all sufficient grace. Paul also makes it clear in verse 12 that the death working in us, is for the sake of getting the life of Christ into others.

What all this means is that the Christian life is not about sitting on a recliner all of our life, but it is about a call to service, no matter how difficult it may be. I think foreign missionaries have to make many sacrifices for the sake of ministering the Gospel. Many acts of service require more prayer and fasting, more faith, more money, longer hours working, many tears shed, and of course, persecution and rejection. But those who accept the call will have a desire to serve, no matter how hard it is. The love and joy of God will abound within, causing them to press on and persevere.

Read 2 Corinthians 6:3-10 and 11:23-29. In these scriptures you will see all the troubles Paul went through for the sake of the Gospel. But this takes us back to 2 Corinthians 7:4 (NIV) where Paul said, "In all my troubles my joy knows no bounds." And 2 Corinthians 12:10 (NIV) reads, "That is why, for Christ's sake, I delight in weaknesses, in insults, in hardships, in persecutions, in difficulties. For when I am weak, then I am strong." I know we do not like to hear too may Words like these today, but this is real grace in action.

How about you? Along with the river of delights, which is real and authentic, will you also accept the call of being given over to death for Christ's sake? Do not respond to this with the natural man that is selfish and fearful, but let the Holy Spirit do a real work in your heart, examining your motives. It is also important not to let this Word get out of balance, whereby we develop a martyr's complex and give in to the enemy.

Jesus said in Matthew 11:12 (NKJV), "The kingdom of heaven suffers violence, and the violent take it by force." We are to get violent against the enemy of God and continue to fight the good fight!

Amen!!!

The Test Of Our Love

Matthew 25:31-46 (NKJV)

This is the famous scripture where Jesus separates the sheep from the goats. The sheep enter into eternal life and the goats into eternal punishment. How you tell the difference between the two is by the test of their love. The test of their love is a confirmation of what James taught in James 2:14-26. So we see in Jesus' Words and James' words that faith without works is dead. Galatians 5:6 (NIV) reads, "The only thing that counts is faith expressing itself through love."

Jesus said in Matthew 25:35-40 (NKJV), "For I was hungry and you gave Me food; I was thirsty and you gave Me drink; I was a stranger and you took Me in; I was naked and you clothed Me; I was sick and you visited Me; I was in prison and you came to Me." "Then the righteous will answer Him, saying, Lord when did we see You hungry and feed You, or thirsty and give You drink? When did we see You a stranger and take You in, or naked and clothed You? Or when did we see You sick or in prison, and come to You? Assuredly, I say to you, inasmuch as you did it to one of the least of these My brethren, you did it to Me."

So how has your love been tested lately? Have you given food or drink to Jesus? Have you given Jesus shelter or clothes? Have you visited Jesus in the hospital or prison? If we ask the Holy Spirit to lead us in this matter, there are many ways to bless Jesus. If we just slow down long enough in our busy lives, and open our eyes and ears we will see and hear the opportunities all around us!

We also need to look at this scripture with a spiritual application as well. Giving food and drink can also be about the food of God's Word and the drink of the Spirit. Offering shelter to a stranger can be about God as a hiding place and refuge. Clothes for the naked can be about being clothed in Christ; putting on the garment of salvation, putting on the full armor of God, and a garment of praise. Then there is ministering to the sick with our prayers, laying on of hands, teaching healing scriptures, and building them up with hope for healing. Lastly, ministering freedom and liberty for those who are oppressed in prisons of darkness.

Those who entered into eternal punishment were the goats on the left who had said in verse 44, "Lord, when did we see You hungry or thirsty or a stranger or naked or sick or in prison, and did not minister to You? Then He will answer them, saying, Assuredly, I say to you, inasmuch as you did not do it to one of the least of these, you did not do it to Me." This is called a sin of omission. James 4:17 (NIV) reads, "Anyone, then, who knows the good he ought to do and doesn't do it, sins."

In our ministry sometimes we have special outreaches to the homeless at a park in Daytona Beach, Florida. We will serve hot food, give out clothes, cut hair, give out flu shots, live music, and preaching of the Gospel. We minister to large crowds the whole day, spirit, soul, and body. At one of these outreaches my wife got some peroxide and bandages, and she was cleaning the blistered feet of a homeless man. He had tears running down his face as she was showing him true love.

We are reminded in these scriptures that any time we minister to a person in Jesus' name, we are also ministering to Jesus as well. Remember this is not a salvation by works, but it is a salvation by faith in His grace that results in works to His honor and glory (Ephesians 2:8-10).

Amen!!!

Your Word Was To Me The Joy And Rejoicing Of My Heart

Jeremiah 15:16 (NKJV) "Your Words were found, and I ate them, and Your Word was to me the joy and rejoicing of my heart."

Jeremiah was ministering to a stubborn and rebellious people. He had a message of judgment against Israel and the nations. The people responded with harsh persecution against him. Jeremiah was depressed and discouraged because of his hard task, but in the midst of it all, God's Word became the joy and rejoicing of his heart.

Notice that Jeremiah 15:16 starts out saying, "Your Words were found." God's Word is never lost! The problem is that many look for answers to their problems in all the wrong places. Are you seeking healing apart from God's Word? Whether it is physical, emotional, sin related, or relational healing, God's Word is the source. Proverbs 12:18b (NIV) reads, "The tongue of the wise brings healing." And Proverbs 10:21a (NIV) reads, "The lips of the righteous nourish many." Those Words of wisdom that bring healing and nourishment come directly from God's Word. It may be a Word directly from God's written Word, which is called "Logos" in the Greek, or it may be a spoken Word from the Holy Spirit and that is called "Rhema" in the Greek. Either way, God's Word will bring joy and rejoicing to the heart. It will be joy to those the Word is intended for and to the person that delivers the Word. Just as Proverbs 11:25b (NIV) reads, "He who refreshes others will himself be refreshed."

In reflecting on the Words of Proverbs 11:25, as we have different problems in our lives and those around us have problems, we bless ourselves the more we look to God for a Word for them as well as ourselves. Proverbs 11:25b (NKJV) reads, "And he who waters will also be watered himself." In Ephesians 5:26 (NKJV) Paul says, "That He might sanctify and cleanse her with the washing of water by the Word." So we see that the Word of God that comes from the fountain of life is like a cool refreshing drink to the soul.

In going back to Jeremiah 15:16, notice that Jeremiah ate the Word. That is a picture of total consumption. We are not to nibble on God's Word, but we are to consume it. The more we consume it, the more delight we will have in God.

Many Christians lose sight of the powerful effect of God's Word. Too much focus on life's problems will cause depression, discouragement, and hopelessness. But the joy and rejoicing that come only by God's Word will change things within. The problems may not change, but your perspective will. So the big question is, what does your spiritual diet consist of?

The more you seek the heart of God, the more you will hear and receive from Him, and thus you will have joy and rejoicing of the heart!

Amen!!!

The Glory Of The Lord

Isaiah 60:1-3 (NIV) "Arise, shine, for your light has come, and the glory of the Lord rises upon you. See, darkness covers the earth and thick darkness is over the peoples, but the Lord rises upon you and His glory appears over you. Nations will come to your light, and kings to the brightness of your dawn."

This is a Word that was prophesied to Israel, but the message of God's glory holds true to all believers in Jesus Christ. Isaiah had seen the glory of the Lord recorded in Isaiah chapter 6, and John 12:41 points out that it was Jesus whom Isaiah had seen. Just as Colossians 1:27 declares that Christ in us is the hope of glory.

Hebrews 1:3 (NIV) reads, "The Son is the radiance of God's glory and the exact representation of His being." We also see in 1 Peter 4:14 and 2 Corinthians 3:17-18 that the Holy Spirit is called the Spirit of glory, and the Spirit is in us and rests upon us. In reference to all these different scriptures we see that the glory of God is revealed in the Father, Son, and Holy Spirit.

The glory is known as His presence, His character, His power, and His beauty. We also see that the glory of God changes us to be more like Him in an ever-increasing fashion. We are changed because His presence is with us and in us, and His presence brings power and beauty into our lives. In Exodus 34:33-35 we see that the face of Moses was radiant due to God's glory. Our faces will also reflect the beauty of His countenance when we spend time with Him.

"Kavod" is a Hebrew word that means "glory". It speaks of a weight or heaviness as God's presence. In Exodus 40:34-35, the glory of God filled the Tent of Meeting and Moses could not enter. He could not enter because the presence of God's glory was so thick, it filled the tabernacle. We see another example of this in 2 Chronicles 5:13-14 where the temple was filled with a cloud, for the glory of the Lord filled the temple.

So not only does man experience the glory of God in His person, but there is a real tangible presence to be experienced in God. This tangible presence of His glory is life changing and will bring man to his knees in submission. The more our churches actually seek the face of God, and welcome His presence with reverence, we will see more powerful results of His presence, such as salvations, healings, miracles, and a freedom in the gifts of the Spirit.

It has been my experience in ministry that sometimes when praying over people they will fall to the ground. I believe this is so because of the glory of God being manifested. I know for myself when I am praying over people or during a worship time that I feel His presence, I feel weak in my legs. Sometimes we can put too much emphasis on people falling down. The real demonstration of the glory of the Lord are the resulting life changing effects that come into our lives.

Referring back to Isaiah 60:1-3, we see that even when darkness covers the earth, the glory of God rises upon us, and thus we will shine as bright lights and be over-comers in the midst of darkness. In these last days we are seeing more and more demonstrations of darkness on the earth, but we are also seeing more demonstrations of the glory of God upon His people.

So as Isaiah said, "Arise, shine, for your light has come." it is time we rise in His presence and power and reflect His brightness for all the earth to see!

Amen!!!

He Continues To Deliver Us

2 Corinthians 1:8-11(NIV)

In these verses of scripture, Paul is expressing to the Church the extreme hardships he and his companions were going through. They literally felt as though death was knocking on the door of their lives. But Paul said in verse 9, "This happened that we might not rely on ourselves but on God."

Many of our major trials in life are meant by God to push us to the point of extreme dependence upon Him. Paul also said in verse 9 that God raises the dead, so Paul believed that God could rescue him from this trial of death that was knocking. Paul also expressed his faith by saying in verse 10, "He has delivered us from such a deadly peril, and he will deliver us. On Him we have set our hope that He will continue to deliver us, as you help us by your prayers."

What we see in Paul's expression of faith is a demonstration of what 2 Corinthians 4:13 (NIV) says, "It is written: I believed; therefore I have spoken. With that same spirit of faith we also believe and therefore speak." Just as Romans 10:6-10 teaches us, that faith speaks and faith is voice activated. When we go through trials in life we need to speak what God's Word says and not speak what the circumstances say. That does not mean that we are in denial of what we are going through, but we're not letting our circumstances dictate the outcome to us. Proverbs 18:21 (NKJV) reads, "Death and life are in the power of the tongue, and those who love it will eat its fruit."

Paul also had hope and faith because God had already delivered him at various times in the past. Just as when David was facing Goliath, David reflected with faith from when God had delivered him from the lion and the bear. Every trial that we go through with victory prepares us for the next trial. We will end up having more and more confidence each time, because great is His faithfulness!

Paul said in verse 10 that the prayers of the saints

helped to bring his deliverance. Paul understood the power of our prayers for one another. In Romans 15:30-32, once again Paul asked for the Church to pray for him in his struggles. Also in Philippians 1:19, Paul mentioned that the prayers of the Church and the help given by the Spirit brought forth his deliverance. James also reminds us of the power of praying saints when he said in James 5:16b (NKJV), "The effective, fervent prayer of a righteous man avails much." To avail much means that the prayers are powerful and get results.

2 Chronicles 20:1-30 is another example of the powerful results of prayer. In this scripture God defeated Judah's enemy because Judah came together corporately to pray and fast, seeking God's help.

What we learn from 2 Corinthians 1:8-11 is to let others know what you are going through and ask for prayer. But do not stop there, continue to proclaim with faith that God is your deliverer, and do not lose hope. Also, reflect on God's resurrection power that abides in you. And if God can raise the dead, He can rescue you! Lastly, reflect on past victories and regain hope and faith in your Holy Spirit reflections.

God will always be glorified and He will bring us through our trials!

Amen!!!

The Great Escape

2 Peter 2:9a (NIV) "The Lord knows how to rescue godly men from trials."

Psalm 34:17 (NIV), "The righteous cry out, and the Lord hears them, He delivers them from all their troubles."

1 Corinthians 10:13 (NKJV), "No temptation has overtaken you except such as is common to man; but God is faithful, who will not allow you to be tempted beyond what you are able, but with the temptation will also make the way of escape, that you may be able to bear it."

Hebrew 1:14 (NIV), "Are not all angels ministering spirits sent to serve those who will inherit salvation."

In God's faithfulness and love, He will rescue, deliver, send angels to help, and provide ways of escape, to His covenant sons and daughters in Christ. He does this more so when we appropriate the blessings of His shed blood, the Spirit, and the Word in our lives.

In Acts 5:17-21, God sent an angel to release the apostles that were in jail. Then again in Acts 12:1-10, God sent an angel to release Peter from jail. In Acts 16:22-28, God caused an earthquake to shake the prison doors, causing Paul and Silas to be released, and the jailer and his family got saved.

In Daniel chapter 6, God delivered Daniel from the lions. In Daniel chapter 3, God delivered Shadrach, Meshach, and Abednego from the fiery furnace. In Exodus chapter 14, Israel was facing the sea in front of them and the Egyptian army behind them, but God opened the sea, and they crossed on dry ground. Listen to the Words of God spoken through Moses. "Do not be afraid. Stand firm and you will see the deliverance the Lord will bring you today. The Egyptians you see today you will never see again. The Lord will fight for you; you need only to be still." (Exodus 14:13-14 NIV).

In 2 Kings 6:8-23, there were angels on chariots of fire all around the enemy, protecting God's people. In 2 Kings 6:24-7:20, God brought a miraculous provision during a time of famine. In Judges chapter 7, God defeated the Midianite army with only 300 men.

Isaiah 43:2-3 (NKJV) reads, "When you pass through the waters, I will be with you; And through the rivers, they shall not overflow you. When you walk through the fire, you shall not be burned, nor shall the flame scorch you. For I am the Lord your God."

These scriptures, and many more like them, are meant to minister hope, faith and encouragement. Just as 1 Peter 4:12 points out, all of us will go through fiery trials, but God is with us. Throughout the Bible, God is consistently saying, "Fear not for I am with you."

Psalm 91:14-16 (NIV) reads, "Because he loves me, says the Lord, I will rescue him; I will protect him, for he acknowledges my name. He will call upon me, and I will answer him; I will be with him in trouble, I will deliver him and honor him. With long life will I satisfy him and show him my salvation." These Words in Psalm 91 are a key part of all of God's rescues. The key is an intimate and loving, faith filled relationship with God.

I pray that whatever trials you face, no matter how big and difficult it may appear, that you can draw some courage from this word of exhortation. To God be the glory!

Amen!!!

Power In His Name

Proverbs 18:10 (NKJV) "The name of the Lord is a strong tower, the righteous run to it and are safe."

Psalm 20:1 (NKJV), "May the Lord answer you in the day of trouble; may the name of the God of Jacob defend you."

Psalm 91:14b (NIV), "I will protect him for he acknowledges my name."

Psalm 124:8 (NIV), "Our help is in the name of the Lord, the Maker of heaven and earth."

Psalm 20:7 (NIV), "Some trust in chariots and some in horses, but we trust in the name of the Lord our God."

There is power in God's name because God is faithful to His promises. In Hebrews 6:13-18, God said that He had sworn to His promises by an oath. His name represents the oath. 2 Corinthians 1:20 (NIV) reads, "For no matter how many promises God has made, they are "Yes" in Christ. And so through Him the "Amen" is spoken to us to the glory of God." Amen means it is finished and complete, a sure thing.

When we run to the name of God, actually we are running to Him. His name represents Himself and His promises. So we can run to His name for protection, healing, provision, strength, and any other promised blessing that we are in need of.

In the Old Testament many different blessings were attached to God's name. Here are a few of them: Jehovah-Shalom, The Lord is peace; Jehovah-Rophe, The Lord heals; Jehovah-Jireh, The Lord provides.

In the New Testament all the blessings of God are in the name of Jesus. Ephesians 1:3 (NIV), "Praise be to the God and Father of our Lord Jesus Christ, who has blessed us in heavenly realms with every spiritual blessing in Christ."

"Therefore God exalted Him to the highest place and

gave Him the name that is above every name, that at the name of Jesus every knee should bow, in heaven and on earth and under earth, and every tongue confess that Jesus Christ is Lord, to the glory of God the Father." (Philippians 2:9-11 NIV). All authority in heaven and earth has been given to Him (Matthew 28:18). Demons tremble at the mention of His name. We pray in His name, cast out demons in His name, heal the sick in His name, and minister in His name. Colossians 3:17 (NIV) reads, "And whatever you do, whether in word or deed, do it all in the name of the Lord Jesus, giving thanks to God the Father through Him."

It is also important to know that the use of God's name is not something to be used by just anyone like it is a magic wand. The story in Acts 19:13-16 teaches us that in order to use the name of God properly and effectively, we must have a relationship with God!

Lastly, we see from David's example in 1 Samuel 17 that we are to fight the good fight of faith with victory in the name of God.

As we grow in our relationship with God, learning His promises, and coming to know the power and authority that is in His name, then we will speak His name with confidence and assurance. With the confidence we gain in His name, we will step out to do great and mighty things in His name. We will not back down from the enemy and we will move forward proclaiming the power of His kingdom!

Amen!!!

What Do You Trust In?

Psalm 20:7 (NIV) "Some trust in chariots and some in horses, but we trust in the name of the Lord our God."

Psalm 108:12-13 (NKJV) "Give us help from trouble, for the help of man is useless. Through God we will do valiantly, for it is He who shall tread down our enemies."

Psalm 147:10-11 (NIV) "His pleasure is not in the strength of the horse, nor his delight in the legs of a man; the Lord delights in those who fear Him, who put their hope in His unfailing love."

The chariots and horses were the strength of an army in ancient days. This would be similar to the strength of an armored tank today, or the power of a fighter jet or missile. As powerful as these different weapons of warfare are, we must remember the battle is the Lord's, and it is in His name that we trust. So a military unit must be prepared as much as possible, but the success lies in the trust and favor of God.

God does not even find pleasure in the strength of man or his weapons, but His delight is in those who trust Him. What pleases God is when man has a reverent awe and respect towards Him. We have a living hope because of the resurrection of Jesus Christ. And our hope is in God's unending and unfailing love.

How do we apply this to our everyday lives? When our country goes to battle, no matter how great our military is, we cannot trust in that alone. Remember pride goes before the fall, and sometimes we have too much pride in the strength of our military, or even in our own strength. Another example is when you are sick and you go to the doctor for medical treatment. Do you trust solely in the doctor or in God? Do you even go to God first in prayer when you are sick? It is okay to seek medical treatment, but let us put our primary trust in God. How about when we seek man's advice and counsel for problems in life? Are God and His Word included in seeking advice? I have always said the best place to receive counsel is to sit in the pew week after week hearing the Word of God taught. Some people will go to a pastor for counsel, but would not even come to church regularly.

Another example is when man puts all his trust for retirement in his portfolio. We have seen in recent years how many have lost thousands in their 401K. Yes, it is good to plan and save financially, but our trust cannot be in money. A natural disaster or major illness could wipe away everything that we have trusted in. So with all of man's wisdom and strength and proper planning in life, God needs to be our chief corner stone, or everything will come tumbling down. It is only a matter of time, when we refuse to trust God, and trust in everything else instead.

Ultimately when death comes knocking, who or what will you trust in? With Jesus Christ as our savior, we can face death with a confident assurance. But without Jesus, death is a fearful thing to face. Everything in life that man has put his trust in will not take away the fear of death. Only God can remove that fear, as we trust in Him.

So who or what are you trusting in your life? I trust in the name of the Lord my God! Through Him I shall do valiantly, for He defeats all my enemies!

Amen!!!

A Continual Feast

Proverbs 15:15 (NIV) "All the days of the oppressed are wretched, but the cheerful heart has a continual feast."

Proverbs 17:22 (NIV), "A cheerful heart is good medicine, but a crushed spirit dries up the bones."

Proverbs 15:13 (NKJV), "A merry heart makes a cheerful countenance, but by sorrow of the heart the spirit is broken."

Each of these verses has a contrasting statement. There is the life of oppression and brokenness, a crushed spirit that is wretched and sorrowful. And there is the life that is cheerful and merry. Each type of life has a continual feast. One will feast on God's grace with His abundant provision of joy. The other will feast on the despair, depression, and discouragements that the devil brings against those whose hearts are not totally surrendered to God.

You are not born with a happy disposition; it takes making the right choices in life to be cheerful. It takes choosing God over self, and it takes choosing to walk in the Spirit as opposed to the lust of the flesh. "Happy are the poor in spirit, for theirs is the kingdom of Heaven." (Matthew 5:3 NIV). Happiness begins when we admit that we are in need of God and that we are not self-sufficient. "Happy is he whose transgressions are forgiven, whose sins are covered." (Psalm 32:1 NIV). Happiness continues when we receive God's forgiveness, by believing on the Lord Jesus Christ. Not only will God make us happy in life, but also He gives us an inner rejoicing of joy in our hearts. We are the ones though, that are encouraged to stir up that joy and keep it active and overflowing in our lives.

Many who are oppressed, are so because they have listened to lies and fears that the devil has whispered into their minds. Some have been bound in oppression for so long, they do not know any other way to live. And sad to say,

"Nor do they know how to get free." And the sorrow that is in their lives affects many around them.

But here is the good news: all can receive the continual feast of joy. No one has to remain bound in oppression and sorrow. The grace of our Lord Jesus Christ and the power of the Holy Spirit can set the captives free and fill them with joy unspeakable.

One time when I was ministering, a woman came up for prayer. She had shared that she recently got a massage and the masseuse was speaking about new age beliefs while massaging her. After the massage, she had felt oppressed and lost her joy. I laid my hands on her head, resisted the spirit of oppression, and she fell down under the power of the Spirit and began laughing nonstop. Needless to say, God set her free and she regained her joy unspeakable. Time and time again I have seen the power of the Holy Spirit set people free and filled them with joy.

If you are going to a church where there is no joy, then I recommend moving on. It is hazardous to your spiritual health. Dead and dry religion will rob you of joy. God gives us joy and wants us to walk in it daily, even when we are in trials. The joy that you choose and tap into will catapult you through your trials.

The question is, "What will you continually feast on?" I have tasted and seen that the Lord is good. No drug or alcohol or any experience in life can compare to the joy of the Lord! I pray, encourage, and challenge you to receive His joy and feast continually. But be forewarned: God's joy is life changing!

Amen!!!

Prayer

Luke 18:1 (NKJV) "Men always ought to pray and not lose heart."

Matthew 6:6 (NKJV) "When you pray, go into your room, and when you have shut your door, pray to your Father who is in the secret place; and your Father who sees in secret will reward you openly."

We always ought to pray, not because it is a religious activity that we must do in order to have God's blessing, but because it keeps us connected with God. Prayer is a gift from God to us as a means of communication. Prayer is not to be a monologue but a dialogue. Prayer is foundational as part of our relationship with God. Not only does God encourage us to talk to Him, but He also wants to talk to us. It is His talking to us that gives us faith and hope, therefore we will not lose heart, but instead we will have heart. When God speaks, not only do we gain faith and hope, but also we gain encouragement, confidence, boldness, and direction.

When Jesus said to go into your room and shut the door when praying, we need to catch the vision of what He is saying. It is in our time of praying regularly that we actually are going through the process of shutting out life's problems. Prayer becomes a safe refuge and shelter insulating us with God's peace. While we are in this place of refuge and shelter, we can refocus our energy towards God, gaining His wisdom and direction, and thus reducing all stress.

The Gospels give us several scenarios of reasons to pray. When we are facing bad news, it is a time to pray. We see that in Matthew 14:13. Jesus had just got word of the death of John the Baptist, and He withdrew to a solitary place. As a result of Jesus getting away to pray after hearing the bad news, He then continued to minister in power, healing the sick, and the miracle of feeding 5,000 with five loaves of bread and two fish.

Another time to pray is when you are tired (Matthew

14:23). Jesus had just ministered all day, and then He went to the mountainside to pray. Ministry will sap your energy spirit, mind and body. I know this from experience, like when I have served on 3-day retreats, or an all day seminar. Recently I went to Honduras and our team started at 8 AM and served to about 6 PM. That was very draining, but prayer refreshed us. Sometimes the refreshing prayer is just sitting still in His presence and receiving.

Mark 1:35 is a reference of Jesus taking time to pray in His busy schedule. Some may say they're too busy to pray. If someone is that busy, then they're too busy not to pray. Our busyness causes us to miss God, therefore we need to pray. Our prayer time will reduce the stress from our busy lives, helping us to refocus, and stay centered in God.

Another time to pray is when we are facing people pressures. In John 6:15 Jesus knew the people wanted to force Him to be king, so He withdrew to a mountain. Most people pressures that we experience are others trying to get us to sin, go against God's leading, and follow the crowd. Sometimes we just need to pull away and pray in a quiet place. We should never make decisions in a hasty environment. It is always good to practice being still before God to hear His direction before making any snap decisions.

In Luke 6:12 we see that Jesus got away to pray before choosing His disciples. So it is always good to pray before making any big decisions. We should pray about our careers, education, marriage, buying a house or car, and the list goes on. Nothing is too big or too small to pray about.

In Matthew 4:1-2 we see that Jesus fasted and prayed before the launching of His ministry. We also see in Acts 13:1-3 that prayer and fasting was an integral part of the launching of Barnabas and Saul into their ministry. Whether it is a big ministry move or something on a smaller scale, prayer should always play a major role in our choices.

Lastly, we see in Matthew 26:39-44 and John 17 that Jesus prayed before facing His cross. We all have crosses to bear and prayer is necessary to face them. In all matters in life, our prayer time is a time to depend upon the Holy Spirit and to receive from Him. So I encourage you to enter that prayer closet daily and shut the door behind you. It will be a glorious habitation in the Lord!

Amen!!!

Prayer

Romans 12:12 (NKJV) "Rejoicing in hope, patient in tribulation, continuing steadfastly in prayer."

1 Thessalonians 5:16-18 (NKJV) "Rejoice always, pray without ceasing, in everything give thanks, for this is the will of God in Christ Jesus for you."

Prayer is a reflection of your devotion to God and His work. Prayer primes the pump for power and fruitfulness in your life and ministry. Prayer should be a discipline in our lives instead of a despairing cry during a time of crisis.

Rejoicing is to be part of our prayer time. Rejoicing is an action word whereby I choose to yield to joy by praising God. As Paul said, "We are to rejoice always and we rejoice in hope." Hope is a positive expectation to receive goodness from God based on His promises. So we see that hope gives us reason to rejoice. Sometimes it takes much effort to rejoice when we are facing trials, but when we do so it helps us to stay focused on God's hope filled promises.

So speaking of God's hope-filled promises, we see that it is important to spend time in the Word of God along with our prayer time. John 15:7 (NKJV) reads, "If you abide in Me, and My Words abide in you, you will ask what you desire, and it shall be done for you." This verse is not meant to be a magic formula to get what you want, but it is centered on knowing God's mind, to pray in accordance with.

"Pray without ceasing" simply means that we are always in an attitude of prayer, being aware of God's presence. We should always have that awareness that God is with us, in us, and for us, and He will never leave us nor forsake us. Prayer is to be like the air you breath, talking to God and Him talking to you, a necessity in life.

Another aspect of our prayer life is to give thanks in all things. In other words, even when something really bad happens in life, we can give thanks to God in the midst of it because God is our hope and strength. He is able to work all things together for our good. That is another one of God's promises that we find in Roman 8:28, but notice that it is connected to verses 26-27 talking about prayer.

As we dissect the order of Romans 12:12 we see that our steadfast prayer life coupled with rejoicing will help us to be patient in tribulation. Patience is the fruit of the Spirit, which already abides within us, and we pull it out through prayer and rejoicing. "Holy Spirit, I yield to patience in this trial. I thank you for the strength to persevere and overcome."

For me, the prayer that primes the pump for power and fruitfulness in my life is praying prostrate on the floor, or sitting still before Him. During this time, I worship and listen, and express my dependence and trust to God.

I pray that this word encourages you to spend more time in prayer with rejoicing and thanksgiving. May you learn God's Word and pray in accordance to it, and may you experience more power and fruitfulness as a result thereof!

Amen!!!

Prayer

Jeremiah 33:3 (NKJV) "Call to Me, and I will answer you, and show you great and mighty things, which you do not know."

Ephesians 3:20 (NKJV) "Now to Him who is able to do exceedingly abundantly above all that we ask or think, according to the power that works in us."

These are two of the most popular verses of scripture on prayer. One was addressed to the nation of Judah while in captivity to Babylon, the other is addressed to the Church of Jesus Christ. Both verses empower us to call upon God, and encourage us to press in with God, and thus we will see powerful results to our prayers.

Jeremiah was in prison when he heard the Holy Spirit speak this Word. There are many today in different types of prisons and the Holy Spirit is calling you to prayer. God wants to show you great and mighty things, things that you cannot even imagine. God continued to speak to Jeremiah saying, "I will bring health and healing to My people, and an abundance of peace and restoration, and cleansing and forgiveness of their sin." God is also saying this today for those who will call upon Him. God's grace reaches out to us all, no matter where we are in life. He is not condemning or accusing, but He is knocking on the door of our hearts. He wants to fellowship with us and impart His love, and thus change us from the inside out.

This Word to Jeremiah and the nation of Judah gives us hope. The fulfillment of this hope begins with us calling upon God, expressing a cry for help with some child-like faith. Only mustard seed size faith is needed to reach out to God. What is big is the deep well of His grace, and our faith is in His grace.

In Ephesians 3:20, Paul points out that God's power and willingness to answer our prayers in immeasurable fashion is based on the power that works in us. The power that works in us is the Holy Spirit. The Holy Spirit first leads us to ask and envision. Our vision comes from God's Word, which creates expectation within us. So not only are we asking but also we are believing and receiving by faith and not by sight. Also, with this Spirit-filled faith, we will speak to mountains in our lives and refuse to doubt. And we will continue to resist the evil one with steadfast faith. We know God has our back as He backs up His Word. The power within us is also a heart filled with love from the Holy Spirit. As we are filled with love, our prayers will come from proper motives, and a vision of God's love intervening through our prayers.

My questions to you are: "Are you praying in the power of the Holy Spirit? Are you praying with vision and expectation, and is your heart filled with God's love?" God is calling you to press in, in your prayer closet. He is saying come up higher on eagle's wings, where you will soar in victory.

We can wallow through life defeated or we can take hold of the gift of prayer and over-come, because God is good and He desires to pour out His goodness in our lives!

Amen!!!

Prayer

Luke 11:5-13, 18:1-8

These scriptures in Luke 11 and Luke 18 are a contrast of how much more God will answer prayers because of His great love for us. These scriptures also speak of persistence, but not a persistence of wearying God and twisting His arm, but a persistence of faith in His grace. Romans 4:16 also speaks of this same truth. Luke 11:8 mentions the man getting up to give his friend as much as he needs because of his boldness. In Luke 18:8 (NIV) Jesus said, "However, when the Son of Man comes, will He find faith on the earth?"

In light of these two stories we see that our faith is not in the religious ritual of prayer. As Jesus said in Matthew 6:7, we are not to pray with vain babbling. Our prayers are about making contact with God. We connect with God when we focus on His love and grace, and not on our religious rituals.

As we approach God with our petitions, we need to see what God has promised concerning such requests. Then, based on God's grace, we ask with thanksgiving. And we continue to give thanks as a way of expressing our faith. Receiving is not about seeing with the natural eyes, but it is about seeing with the eyes of the Spirit.

In reflecting on the man's boldness in Luke 11:8, how much more can we expect to receive when we pray in Jesus' name. Ephesians 3:12 and Hebrew 4:14-16 clearly teach us that we can receive from God's throne of grace, and we can approach Him with confidence and boldness. The shed blood of Jesus is what grants us this access with boldness.

Will Jesus find faith on earth when He returns? The kind of faith that Jesus is talking about is persistent faith. Persistent faith is standing firm in God's grace without wavering and being double-minded. We are to keep our focus on His love and faithfulness, and not doubt His promises. The more we hear God's Word and listen to the Holy Spirit, the more faith we will have to apply to our life of prayer.

Luke 11:13 (NIV) reads, "If you then, though you are evil, know how to give good gifts to your children, how much more will your Father in heaven give the Holy Spirit to those who ask Him!" The way this verse is worded in the Greek means how much more will your Father in heaven give the works, manifestations, grace and power of the Holy Spirit. In other words, whatever the need, we can ask and it is the Holy Spirit that imparts.

Just as 2 Peter 1:3 (NIV) says, "His divine power has given us everything we need for life and godliness through our knowledge of Him." Actually what we need is in the Holy Spirit, and it is about yielding more so than asking. In 2 Peter 1:3 when it says, "Through our knowledge of Him", it is speaking of Jesus and what He has provided for us through the cross and resurrection, which is the cornerstone of His gift of grace.

In summary, we see all of our prayers are to be centered in God's grace. That is what our faith is in, and where our faith comes from. It is this faith that comes by grace that gives us boldness, causing us to be persistent!

Amen!!!

Have You Received The Holy Spirit?

Acts 19:1-7

In reading this text Paul had asked some disciples, "Did you receive the Holy Spirit when you believed?" There are a couple of interpretations and explanations of what these verses mean, depending on your church background. But I have a thought as to how these verses apply to you, regardless of your explanation of these verses of scripture.

The question is not whether or not the Holy Spirit is in you, because we know from Romans 8:9 that if you are born-again, the Spirit is in you. The real question is, "Are you receptive of the Holy Spirit in your life?" Are you receptive of His working in you? Are you receptive of the fruit of the Spirit? Are you receptive of the gifts of the Spirit? Are you receptive of His leading, power and control in your life? Are you receptive of Him as your prayer partner and ministry partner? Are you receptive of Him as your teacher and counselor? All these questions boil down to a relationship with the Holy Spirit.

When you look at the question in this context, then I ask you again, "Have you received the Holy Spirit?" Another way to explain Paul's question is simply, "Are you filled with the Holy Spirit, or living the Spirit-filled life?" There are many truly born-again Christians that are not living the Spirit-filled life. For some it is due to ignorance. They have not been taught about the Holy Spirit or learned yet on their own. Sad to say there are many preachers that do not know the Holy Spirit, and that is why their churches are dead, dry, and boring.

Then there are many who do know the Holy Spirit and are receptive of Him in their lives, but they limit Him to a degree. Once again, that is usually due to what people have been taught and they try to put God in a box, so to speak.

The Holy Spirit is much bigger than our peanut brains can comprehend. We need to make sure we do not quench and limit Him due to our natural reasoning and understanding. In Ephesians 1:17-19 (NIV) we see Paul's prayer, "I keep asking that the God of our Lord Jesus Christ, the glorious Father, may give you the Spirit of wisdom and revelation, so that you may know Him better. I pray also that the eyes of your heart may be enlightened in order that you may know the riches of His glorious inheritance in the saints, and His incomparably great power for us who believe. That power is like the working of His mighty strength."

It is only by divine revelation that we fully understand and yield to all the different workings of the Holy Spirit. So I encourage you to pray Paul's prayer for yourself and others. Ask the Father to speak to you by His Spirit, and accept what God's Word says. Do not water it down with your reasoned excuses as why it is not for you today. The Holy Spirit is the same today as He was in yesteryear. Whatever powerful moves of the Spirit that we see in the Book of Acts, are still for today as well. If you press in to God in your prayer closet and study of the Word, and have a genuine thirst to receive, He will fill you overflowing!

In Acts 19:6 (NIV), "When Paul placed his hands on them, the Holy Spirit came on them, and they spoke in tongues and prophesied." The Holy Spirit still comes on people and fills them with tongues and prophecy today. One of the reasons why we do not see it much is because it is not preached and taught, and worse yet it is taught against. And sad to say for many, they are not experiencing any Holy Spirit power in their lives.

How about you? Will you press in and receive? Will you welcome the Holy Spirit into your life to have His way with you, in you, and through you? God is doing great and mighty things on the earth today, and He wants to do them through you as well, but only if you welcome Him. Ask big, believe big, and receive big, and God will do great and mighty things through you!

"No eye has seen, nor ear has heard, no mind has conceived what God has prepared for those who love Him, but God has revealed it to us by His Spirit." (1 Corinthians 2:9-10 NIV).

Amen!!!

Why Tongues?

There is much confusion and misunderstanding in the Church today on the subject of speaking in tongues. Many try to comprehend the subject with natural human reasoning. Here again it is only by divine revelation from the Holy Spirit that we can understand spiritual things. In 1 Corinthians 2:10-15, Paul explains the ministry of the Holy Spirit helping us to discern spiritual truths. Even with that being said, many Christians still use human logic to try to discern spiritual truths. May the Holy Spirit reveal some truth to us through this word of exhortation!

We first see recorded in Acts 2:1-12, that tongues came on the 120 in the upper room on the day of Pentecost. This was part of the initial filling of the Holy Spirit for them. The crowd of people in Jerusalem that day were from different countries and they each heard the 120 speaking the wonders of God in their native languages. God definitely used this to get their attention. Then Peter began to preach the Gospel in the common language that they all understood. I have heard testimonies of someone speaking in a tongue from the Holy Spirit and a person near them heard the tongue and understood what was being said, because it was in their natural tongue. God used that to speak a message to them as well. What we see here in Acts chapter 2 is not an isolated occurrence, nor is it the only way tongues are used.

We also see in Acts 10:44-46 that Gentile believers received the Holy Spirit and spoke in tongues, and again in Acts 19:6 when Paul placed his hands on some disciples, and they received the Holy Spirit, speaking in tongues. In Acts 8:17-19, Peter and John placed their hands on new converts and they received the Holy Spirit. It does not say that they spoke in tongues, but there had to have been some kind of external manifestation, because something got Simon's attention in this matter.

Speaking in tongues and interpretation of tongues are listed in 1 Corinthians 12:10 as spiritual gifts from the Holy

Spirit. Paul also taught on this subject in 1 Corinthians 14, in order to give some clear direction to the Church. 1 Corinthians 12:31 (NIV) reads, "But eagerly desire the greater gifts." The greater gifts are the ones that are in need at the moment. 1 Corinthians 14:1 (NIV) reads, "Follow the way of love and eagerly desire spiritual gifts, especially the gift of prophecy." We see it is encouraged by the Holy Spirit to desire His gifts, not just to say, "If God wants me to speak in tongues, then it will happen." Anything we receive and operate in from the Holy Spirit is out of thirst and desire. Also, Paul said in 1 Corinthians 14:39 (NIV), "Therefore my brothers, be eager to prophesy, and do not forbid speaking in tongues." How many churches today forbid speaking in tongues? Paul also said in 1 Corinthians 14:18-19 (NIV), "I thank God that I speak in tongues more than all of you. But in the church I would rather speak five intelligible words to instruct others than ten thousand words in a tongue." By Paul's statement we see that tongues was a big part of his life and ministry, but there is a proper place for it, which I believe Paul was referring to his prayer time.

I think many take the Acts 2 example and try to explain tongues from that specific occurrence, here again using human logic, and they do not see the need for it today. There are two types of tongues that the Holy Spirit gives. Knowing the difference between the two helps bring a lot of clarity, and removes much of the confusion.

Based on Paul's teaching in 1 Corinthians 14 and 12:10, we see that someone can speak in a tongue with an interpretation to follow, and thus it becomes a prophetic Word. Also, as we saw in Acts chapter 2, someone may hear you speak in their native language that you had not learned. Both of these examples are one way that tongues are used as a form of prophecy. I believe this is what Paul was referring to when he said in 1 Corinthians 12:30 (NIV), "Do all speak in tongues?" In other words, no, all do not operate in this type of tongue.

The other way tongues are used in the Church is in our

prayer closets. Based on 1 Corinthians 14:2, 14-15, we see that speaking in an unlearned tongue by the Holy Spirit is another way to pray. My spirit is praying in connection with the Holy Spirit. And I can sing with my spirit in tongues. Many times when I have a burden to pray for someone, and I am not sure what to pray, I will pray in tongues. Sometimes the Holy Spirit will give me revelation after praying in tongues, but even if not, the Spirit still takes those prayers to the Father.

Also, 1 Corinthians 14:4 (NKJV) reads, "He who speaks in a tongue edifies himself." That means that spiritually you are building yourself up, like a spiritual exercise. When you are down and discouraged, an excellent way to build yourself up is to pray in tongues and sing in tongues. Jude 1:20 (NIV) reads, "But you, dear friends, build yourselves up in your most holy faith and pray in the Holy Spirit." I believe this is also referring to praying in tongues. We build ourselves up and stir ourselves up in many of the spiritual graces that God gives us, so let us not neglect this grace through ignorance.

1 Corinthians 1:18-19 (NIV), "For the message of the cross is foolishness to those who are perishing, but to us who are being saved it is the power of God. For it is written: I will destroy the wisdom of the wise; the intelligence of the intelligent I will frustrate." And 1 Corinthians 1:25 (NIV), "For the foolishness of God is wiser than man's wisdom, and the weakness of God is stronger than man's strength." I believe these same truths here would apply to the subject of tongues too. There are some things in God you just accept by faith, and you do not try to logically figure it out.

A friend of mine had his first experience at speaking in tongues while in the shower. He said that the Holy Spirit told him to pray for his pastor. Then the Holy Spirit said, "Pray in tongues" He responded, "I don't pray in tongues or believe in it." The Holy Spirit said again, "Pray in tongues." At that moment he experienced an overwhelming surge from deep within him and he began to speak in tongues profusely. After showering, he called his pastor to see what was going on during that time. His pastor shared how he was counseling a married couple that was ready to give up and divorce. The pastor did not know what more he could say to them after already trying. It was right then during the praying in tongues in the shower that they, all of a sudden, looked at each other and decided to make it work. Praise God, for His immeasurable wisdom and power!

Another friend of mine had struggled for years with alcoholism. He was saved but he continued on this roller coaster ride of falling with the alcohol about every 30 days. One day he was filled with the Holy Spirit with speaking in tongues, and that began his upward victory over the struggle with alcohol. He has been sober for about 30 years, and along with the many graces of God, he also taps into the grace of praying in tongues regularly.

I encourage you to tap into this grace from the Holy Spirit. Ask God to fill you, and desire to receive. He will fill you! Separate yourself from all the teachings that speak against tongues, and let the Holy Spirit give you revelation. Tongues will bring power into your prayer life and build you up when you need it. Make sure you do not neglect the gift, but put it to use for the glory of God!

Amen!!!

Where's The Power?

Acts 1:8 (NKJV) "But you shall receive power when the Holy Spirit has come upon you; and you shall be witnesses to Me in Jerusalem, and in all Judea and Samaria, and to the end of the earth."

There once was a commercial many years ago that had an old lady saying, "Where's the beef", as she was looking at a puny piece of meat on a bun. It was a funny commercial that got the point across.

In order to get a point across in the Church, we need to ask, "Where's the power?" There's a lot of religion with ritual and tradition, but is there power in our churches today? There are a lot of programs and activities in our churches, but is there any power?

Power needs to start from the pastor in the pulpit. Is he proclaiming the Gospel with power, and is he teaching the church how to receive power, and how to live and minister in power? Are people getting saved at the church services? 1 Thessalonians 1:5 (NIV) reads, "Because our gospel came to you not simply with words, but also with power, with the Holy Spirit and with deep conviction." The power of the Holy Spirit gets results. It gets results in us and through us.

This word power in the Greek is "dunamis", which is where we get the word dynamite. It is the life changing power of God. Dunamis changed Peter from being a rugged fisherman that was impulsive, to a powerful preacher of the Gospel. Dunamis fills you with love to serve, boldness to preach, and passion to pray. Dunamis can also be described as the fire of God (1 Thessalonians 5:19), whereby your heart is set ablaze with passion and desire to do the work of the kingdom.

When you have the power of God, you are willing to be a witness. Witness is also translated as martyr. So in other words, with God's power you will witness even unto death, if necessary. And you will die to self and live unto God as a living sacrifice.

Acts 8:1 (NIV) reads, "On that day a great persecution broke out against the church at Jerusalem, and all except the apostles were scattered." And Acts 8:4 (NIV) reads, "Those who had been scattered preached the Word wherever they went." Some will say, "I'm not called to witness; that's not my gift." Well, we see here in Act 8 that everyone was preaching the Gospel when they were scattered. You do not have to preach sermons or have the knowledge of a scholar, but we are all called to witness. The real question is, "Do you have the power of the Holy Spirit?" or "Are you obeying the Holy Spirit?" Just as Joel prophesied in Acts 2:17 (NIV), "In the last days, God says, I will pour out My Spirit on all people. Your sons and daughters will prophesy." The Holy Spirit makes us a mouthpiece for God, and we will speak with power. Many need a personal day of Pentecost!

When the 120 were filled with the Holy Spirit on the day of Pentecost, they were in prayer ready to receive. When the 12 in Acts 19:6 received the Holy Spirit, hands were laid on them. And when the Gentiles received the Holy Spirit in Acts 10:44-46, they were listening attentively to Peter preach. If we are thirsty to receive the power of the Holy Spirit into our lives, we will pray with an expectancy to receive, we will listen attentively to God's Word, and we will not neglect the laying on of hands. God can fill you powerfully through anyone of these ways.

So how about you? Are you ready for a personal day of Pentecost? Are you ready to be filled with power, and become a life-changing vessel of God to a lost and dying world?

"Father, I pray for those reading this word, that they would be filled with dunamis right this moment. I thank you for your faithfulness to empower your people. In Jesus' name!"

Amen!!!

Be Filled With The Spirit

Ephesians 5:18 (KJV) "And be not drunk with wine, wherein is excess; but be filled with the Spirit."

The tense of the verb, "Be filled" in the Greek is a present imperative. That means the verb is not a one-time action, but a continuous action. It could be read as keep on being filled, a continuous filling of the Spirit. If I were to fill a glass of water to the brim, you might say it is filled. But in relation to the filling of the Spirit, I would keep on pouring water into the glass, and thus it would overflow. That is what God wants to do in our lives overflow filling. In John 7:37-39 Jesus spoke of the Holy Spirit in us as rivers of living water.

So that means we cannot live off of yesterday's experience in the Holy Spirit. Everyday I must seek Him first and yield to Him in all things. Sometimes people have a mountain top experience in God, and they keep reflecting on that experience, instead of being filled today. Eventually the memories of that experience will no longer have any effect in you.

We can create our own unique experiences in God everyday. As we start everyday with prayer and worship and Bible reading, yielding to the Holy Spirit, we will overflow. Just stop and imagine the power in a river. And we have the power of rivers of living water. That speaks of refreshing new life, joy, peace and healing. We are to be vessels of this power flowing into us and through us to others, just like Jesus did. Everyday I am sensitive to whom God may have me minister to, or to pray for. That in itself is experiencing God uniquely everyday.

If I am to continue to be filled to overflowing, that means the source never runs dry. There's no limit to the joy I can experience. So when I feel down, I begin to pray and worship and stir up that joy. When I feel the pressures in life, I can yield to the abundant provision of peace. Notice it is about you and me yielding everyday, at all times, and in all situations. I must yield to the power of the Holy Spirit, His control and leading.

To yield, means I will obey and walk by faith, not by sight. It also means that I will rest in the finished work of Jesus on the cross, and rest and trust in the Holy Spirit. I will have a conscious awareness of the presence and power of the Holy Spirit at all times.

In the Spirit-filled life, we can and will have many different experiences. There is the fruit of the Spirit, and there is the operation of the different gifts of the Spirit. There will be different scenarios in our acts of service, and different people. We can also experience the presence of God in our lives in different ways. Notice in Acts 2, the 120 were first filled with the Holy Spirit. Then in Acts 4:24-31 many of them were filled again. It is exciting to live the Spirit-filled life, even in the midst of persecution and attacks from the enemy. It is exciting to see what God will do in you and through you differently everyday.

The devil wants to stop us from being filled daily, but if we stay filled daily, we will continue to overcome anything he sends against us. The devil is no match for the Holy Spirit. So as Paul said in Ephesians 6:10 (KJV), "Be strong in the Lord, and in the power of His might."

Ephesians 5:18 and 6:10 are actually commands to Christians. There is no excuse not to be filled, and there is no excuse not to be strong, to persevere and over-come.

Psalm 23:5 (KJV) reads, "Thou preparest a table before me in the presence of mine enemies: Thou anointest my head with oil; my cup runneth over." Oil is symbolic of the Holy Spirit, so this verse is a picture of the blessing of the Spirit-filled life. It speaks of abundance and fullness.

I pray that your cup is running over and that you yield to being filled daily!

Amen!!!

Bold Prayers Get Bold Results

Acts 4:29-32 (NKJV) "Now, Lord, look on their threats, and grant to Your servants that with all boldness they may speak your Word, by stretching out Your hand to heal, and that signs and wonders may be done through the name of Your holy Servant Jesus. And when they had prayed, the place where they were assembled together was shaken; and they were all filled with the Holy Spirit, and they spoke the Word of God with boldness."

Acts 4:33 (NKJV) "And with great power the apostles gave witness to the resurrection of the Lord Jesus. And great grace was upon them all."

Acts 5:12, 14-16 (NKJV) "And through the hands of the apostles many signs and wonders were done among the people." "And believers were increasingly added to the Lord, multitudes of both men and women, so that they brought the sick out into the streets and laid them on beds and couches, that at least the shadow of Peter passing by might fall on some of them. Also a multitude gathered from the surrounding cities to Jerusalem, bringing sick people and those tormented by unclean spirits, and they were all healed."

We see a powerful sequence of events that was the result of some bold prayers. After receiving threats not to preach the name of Jesus, the apostles decided to pray for even more boldness, so that they could keep on preaching, regardless of the opposition. We see their sequence of events going from prayer, to being filled with boldness, to powerful proclamation, to men and women saved, to signs and wonders, healings, and freedom from tormenting spirits.

Many want to see the powerful results, but are we bold enough to pray such prayers? Are we willing to open our mouths with such proclamations in the face of demonic opposition? The apostles were used as vessels for miracles and healings because they spoke boldly, no holding back! Mark 16:20 (NKJV) reads, "And they went out and preached everywhere, the Lord working with them and confirming the Word through the accompanying signs." God will confirm His Word with powerful results! He does not bring powerful results to tradition and ritual, or when we speak out of fear and doubt. So in order to pray such bold prayers, there needs to be a willingness to obey and follow through in the power of the Holy Spirit.

As we pray such prayers, we need to be faithful where God plants us. And be faithful to every opportunity we have to share the good news. We need to share with people that God loves them, that there is forgiveness through the cross, healing in Jesus' name, and freedom from the tormenting spirits. As we are faithful to share, then and only then, will we see powerful results, such as salvations, healings, and deliverance!

I challenge you and encourage you to pray bold prayers, being inspired and led by the Holy Spirit. Pray for boldness daily and look for opportunities to share and minister the grace of God. Those who are daring to pray bold prayers are those who will see real demonstrations of the power of the Spirit!

How about you? Are you up to the challenge? God is calling on you and He is counting on you. Are you counting on Him?

Amen!!!

Devote Yourselves To Prayer

Ephesians 6:18-20 (NIV) "And pray in the Spirit on all occasions with all kinds of prayers and request. With this in mind, be alert and always keep on praying for all the saints. Pray also for me, that whenever I open my mouth, words may be given me so that I will fearlessly make known the mystery of the gospel, for which I am an ambassador in chains. Pray that I may declare it fearlessly as I should."

Colossians 4:2-6 (NIV) "Devote yourselves to prayer, being watchful and thankful. And pray for us, too, that God may open a door for our message, so that we may proclaim the mystery of Christ, for which I am in chains. Pray that I may proclaim it clearly, as I should. Be wise in the way you act toward outsiders, make the most of every opportunity. Let your conversation be always full of grace, seasoned with salt, so that you may know how to answer everyone."

Both of these exhortations by Paul are very similar. He mentions that we are to be watchful and alert as we pray for one another. Things in our lives that we may not see, the Spirit sees, and will show another for the purpose of interceding, and thus our blind side is protected. Therefore we see the need for praying for one another. Sometimes as I am praying for someone, the Spirit will show me things in their life, and give me a prophetic Word for them. 1 Samuel 12:23 (NIV) reads, "As for me, far be it from me that I should sin against the Lord by failing to pray for you. And I will teach you the way that is good and right." We need one another as a team, and as the body of Christ, in order to function properly, to the highest degree.

In these two scriptures, we see the need for intercession and evangelism in support of the common purposes of God. Paul asked for specific prayers in the area of having the right Words from God in communicating the Gospel, and that it would be communicated with fearlessness and clarity. He also asked for prayer to open doors to share the Gospel. If the Church would pray those prayers daily and weekly for one another, I believe we would see revival in the land and across the world. I challenge every one of you to start praying like that.

Paul also mentions that he is an ambassador in chains, and he is still busy about the Father's business. How about you? Are you about the Father's business? What so called difficulties are holding you back? In both Words Paul said, "As I should." There are no excuses; we are all called to share the Gospel in one way or another. We are all called ambassadors, meaning we represent the King of Glory with His message of salvation to the entire world. And we represent with His power and authority.

In Paul's Word to the Colossians, he reminds us that our witness is also communicated through our actions and how we speak to others, which is to be full of grace. He also mentioned that we should make the most of every opportunity. If that were to be our goal in life, we would actually experience more divine providential interactions with people. But instead we have the tendency to go through life fast, missing those God moments!

Let me summarize Paul's prayer request: Words given, fearlessly proclaim, open doors to share, proclaim it clearly, to be wise in the way we act, make the most of every opportunity, let your conversation be full of grace and salt, and know how to answer everyone.

I encourage and challenge you to devote yourself to prayer. And as we pray for and with one another, let us also go together and share the good news of the Gospel. We must be about our Father's business!

Amen!!!

House Of Prayer

Matthew 21:13-16 (NIV) "It is written," He said to them, "My house will be called a house of prayer, but you are making it a den of robbers." The blind and the lame came to Him at the temple, and he healed them. But when the chief priest and the teachers of the law saw the wonderful things he did and the children shouting in the temple area, "Hosanna to the Son of David," they were indignant. "Do you hear what these children are saying?" they asked Him. "Yes" replied Jesus, "have you never read, 'From the lips of children and infants You have ordained praise?'"

Jesus had cleared the temple once early in His ministry, as recorded in John 2:12-17. In John's reference, Jesus was outraged that they had turned His Father's house into a marketplace. In the other Gospels, Jesus cleared the temple at the end of His ministry. His attitude was the same, He had zeal for His Father's house, but the merchants had turned it into a place of dishonest business. How often are the churches throughout the land used for everything but a house of prayer?

It is notable to see that after Jesus cleansed the temple and announced that it is to be a house of prayer that the blind and lame came to Him at the temple and were healed. I believe if our churches would open their doors for prayer, and have more prayer meetings that we would see more powerful demonstrations of the Spirit. Those miraculous healings are powerful and awesome, but what is needed even more are lives healed and restored in God. We could even have prayer meetings in our homes and places of business. I challenge all business owners to have prayer meetings at lunch and after work, and even invite ministers in occasionally to minister to your employees. There have been revivals in the past, from business people having prayer meetings.

The children were shouting praises unto Jesus. This is

another powerful result of a house of prayer—our children learn to pray and worship. God has ordained praise to come from their lips. They should never be neglected in our worship, but included.

The religious leaders were indignant when all this was going on. The spirit of religion rejects sincere prayer and praise, and thus they will not see any demonstrations of power either. In Luke 19:40 (NIV) after the Pharisees had told Jesus to rebuke the crowd from praising Him, he replied, "I tell you, if they keep quiet, the stones will cry out." All of God's creation was made to bring glory to Jesus. It is important that we do not see church as a religious thing we must do to appease God, but that God's house is a place of prayer, worship and healing!

When we come together in God's house of prayer, as we seek His face, we will experience His forgiveness and healing. He will also use us as the vessels of His healing. Prayer and worship welcome the presence and power of the Holy Spirit, and we will see the spiritual gifts in operation ministering to one another. The more we seek after God with all our hearts, thirsting after Him; we will see Holy Spirit power with lives changed!

Amen!!!

An Expected End

Jeremiah 29:11-14 KJV "For I know the thoughts that I think toward you, saith the Lord, thoughts of peace, and not of evil, to give you an expected end. Then shall ye call upon me, and ye shall go and pray unto me, and I will hearken unto you. And ye shall seek me, and find me, when ye shall search for me with all your heart. And I will be found of you, saith the Lord: and I will turn away your captivity."

This was a Word spoken to Judah during their years of captivity to Babylon. Even though it was a specific Word to them, it still speaks the heart of God to all today. God's thoughts are much higher than our thoughts, and we must never exalt our thoughts above His, or else such becomes idolatry. "How precious to me are your thoughts, O God! How vast is the sum of them! Were I to count them, they would outnumber the grains of sand." (Psalm 139:17-18 NIV). May God's thoughts and our thoughts flow in unity by the Holy Spirit!

God's thoughts are His ways and plans. God's thoughts and plans are for peace and prosperity. Real prosperity is about our whole person, spirit, soul, and body being affected by God in complete wholeness. Peace in Hebrew is "shalom", meaning wholeness. Isaiah 53:5 (NIV) says, "The punishment that brought us peace was upon Him." That verse is speaking of Jesus bearing the punishment for us to have wholeness. Real prosperity is also us being like Jesus in all ways, full of the Spirit.

God's thoughts and plans are not for evil or harm, but for goodness and blessing. There will be times where we wonder if that is true, but even in those times, what appears evil is designed for good. In those trying and difficult times, God will always be doing a work within you to be more like Christ! God is faithful. Trust in His faithfulness!

Within God's thoughts are plans to give us hope and a

future, or an expected end. In the original text of Jeremiah 29:11, it reads, "to give you an end, and expectation." In other words, God's people can expect an end to bad situations in life. God will remove all shame and despair. He will remove your fears and isolation. He will turn sadness into rejoicing, mourning into dancing, weakness into strength. God gives us an expectation by His Word and Spirit. We do not have to lose hope, for God is the God of hope. He wants us to expect and to receive. Jeremiah's Word continues with exhortation to pray, and seek, and search after God with all your heart. And people will do so when they have the hope of an end, and expectation. May our churches have a spirit of expectation at every meeting! God wants to pour out from the floodgates of heaven, but it is in proportion to our seeking and expecting.

This spirit of expectation will come as a result of preaching the Word of God. In hearing of God's love and goodness, and His Almighty power, an expectation is created. The more we are in the atmosphere of Holy Spirit faith, the more our thermostat will move upward.

The ultimate end, and expectation is seen in Revelation 21:3-5 (NKJV), "And I heard a loud voice from heaven saying, 'Behold, the tabernacle of God is with men, and He will dwell with them, and they shall be His people. God Himself will be with them and be their God. And God will wipe away every tear from their eyes; there shall be no more death, nor sorrows, nor crying. There shall be no more pain, for the former things have passed away.' Then He who sat on the throne said, 'Behold, I make all things new.' And He said to me, 'Write, for these words are true and faithful.'"

As we read Hebrews chapter 11, the hall of fame of faith, there were some that did not receive here on earth, but they were still noted for their faith, and they still received, being with God in heaven!

Amen!!!

Mutually Encouraged By Each Other's Faith

Romans 1:11-12 (NIV) "I long to see you so that I may impart to you some spiritual gift to make you strong—that is, that you and I may be mutually encouraged by each other's faith."

Each of us has a spiritual gift or gifts, and as we faithfully yield to those gifts, we will minister strength and faith to one another.

Paul was well aware of this truth, and he lived his life in this revelation. Paul was always longing to minister to someone, especially his fellow believers that he knew. Ministry was the joy and purpose of his life that brought him fulfillment. I would have to say that I live my life in the same way. I am always looking for the ministry opportunities all around me. I look with my natural eyes and my spiritual eyes, and I listen with natural ears and my spiritual ears. The joy of my life is to share Jesus with others in one way or another. It could be my prayers, my words, or my actions of love.

In speaking this truth, Paul was confident in the Holy Spirit to always minister through him. Each of you can also have this confidence in the Holy Spirit, which is what you were created for! We need to realize that each of us has something to minister to one another, making each other strong. I challenge you to get in the habit of asking God, what He would have you do each week at church, to whom can you be a blessing, and in what way. Then go to church looking, being sensitive to the Holy Spirit's leading. Next, live your life like that every day. It will bring fresh joy and purpose into your life. It will help you step out of depression and boredom.

Let your words edify and not tear down. Speak words of comfort, strength, and hope. Give someone a hug and pray an affirming prayer over him or her. Laugh and play with the children. Let it be known through your actions that you are approachable and loveable.

The flip side of this is to let others minister to you also. Do not reject someone from praying with you, and learn to be transparent. Let people see that you have needs too. If you act proud and reject ministry to yourself then you quench the Holy Spirit in others for what they were created to do, and you quench the Holy Spirit from blessing you. God's mode of operation is through the Church body! Romans 1:11-12 points out what true fellowship is all about, which is being connected and building each other up in faith.

In our time of fellowship, we should share what God has been doing in our lives. We can share what we have been reading in the Bible and what God has been teaching us. We can also share how God has been using us in ministry. As we share in this way, we are mutually encouraging one another in the faith. Our sharing may communicate joy, hope, courage, healing and victories. All of this kind of fellowship will always minister strength and faith to one another. There are a few men in my life with whom I always look forward to fellowshiping, because we will be mutually encouraged by each other's faith. We make one another strong. I encourage you to get in the habit of having this kind of fellowship in your life. You would not regret it.

"He who refreshes others will himself be refreshed." (Proverb 11:25b NIV). Paul also made mention of being refreshed (Romans 15:32).

As we yield to our call and gifts and fellowship with true love, being transparent in our faith, we will always refresh one another!

Amen!!!

How Strong Are You?

Proverbs 24:10 (NIV) "If you falter in times of trouble, how small is your strength!"

Proverbs 24:10 (NKJV) "If you faint in the day of adversity, your strength is small."

James 1:12 (NIV) "Blessed is the man who perseveres under trial, because when he has stood the test, he will receive the crown of life that God has promised to those who love Him."

Adversity will always test our character and strength. The test of how strong is one's faith, is revealed in adverse situations. Do we respond to difficulties in life with peace or anxiety, courage or fear, faith or doubt, joy or despair, perseverance or fainting? When a bridge is built, it will be tested with a load of weight before it is ready for use. The same is true in our lives as well. More than anything, our testing is for us to see how strong we really are.

In most of my adult life, I was involved in power lifting, and the way my strength was put to the test was to max out with a heavier weight. A few years ago I took up running, and I was always pushing myself to run farther and faster, to increase my endurance for a race. Similarly, not only will adversity test our strength, but it will also help to strengthen us as it is used to drive us to God, to trust in Him and to yield to Him.

Notice James 1:12 mentions that the one who perseveres is one who has stood the test. In other words, persevering people are remaining steadfast in their faith, steadfast in the Holy Spirit, steadfast in prayer, and steadfast in the garment of praise. They are standing firm, immovable, and unshakeable, because they know who they are in Christ and what they have in Christ. They also know to whom they belong—God Almighty. We are His sons and daughters, His chosen generation to declare His praises. God will always be faithful to us; therefore we are to remain faithful to Him!

Our strength will also be tested in the realm of God stretching us. God will stretch us to do new things in ministry that we have never done before. During those times God would say to you, "Rest and relax in Me and enjoy the ride. Watch and see the great things I will do through you!" Do you want to remain safe in your comfort zones or will you get out of the boat and walk on water?

No one becomes super strong over night; we all go through a process of growth until the day we die. So do not compare yourself with others and do not condemn yourself. God does not condemn you. He always encourages us in our growth. The main thing is to keep making steady progress. Do not get stuck in a rut. This is one of the devil's tactics. So be wise to it.

Notice again in James 1:12 the persevering person does so because of his or her love for God. We must tap into our love relationship with God. Faith works by love (Galatians 5:6). And love is revealed through our obedience. If it is not love then it is religion. If what we have is religion then we will falter and faint in every trial. If what we have is a real relationship with God, yielding to His power and promises, we will persevere!

Amen!!!

You're Only As Strong As Your Weakest Link!

According to Song of Solomon 2:15, it is the little foxes that spoil the vine. In other words, it is the little things in our lives that we ignore or deny that eat away at our lives. It is like a worm destroying a harvest of fruit. Or the little fox eating one grape at a time. It is time that the Church opens her eyes to the slumbering affect of the little things. As Paul said in 1 Corinthians 5:6 (NIV), "A little yeast works through the whole batch of dough." Paul said this in correlation to some sexual immorality taking place in the Church that was being ignored. He basically rebuked them for their actions or lack thereof.

When we consider this topic, it is not just about areas in our lives where we sin or have weakness and constant struggles. But it can also be where we need some refining in our lives, walking more in the fruit of the Spirit and living our lives with a spirit of excellence. We need to check our attitudes and motives according to the Holy Spirit and the Word of God. God may want to stretch you so you can be more mature and complete, not lacking anything. Not lacking anything is in reference to God's character in us and growing in the grace and knowledge of Jesus Christ, full of wisdom.

What kind of steward are you with your time and money? Do you waste time and energy on foolish things in this life? Do you waste your life away in front of the television or in hot pursuit of meaningless hobbies? Yes, God gives us all good things to enjoy in life, but have they become an obsession? What do you invest your money into? Any kingdom purposes?

"Every branch that bears fruit He prunes, that it may bear more fruit." (John 15:2 NKJV). Also in John 15:5 Jesus wants us to bear much fruit, and in John 15:16 Jesus wants us to bear fruit that remain, last and endure. Pruning is the removal of anything dead, diseased, or injured. It is also the removal of old flowers in order to create new growth. God's source of pruning is His Word, according to John 15:3. Now if we do not respond to God's Word, we may have to suffer some negative circumstances in life, not because God made them happen, but because we are reaping what we have sown, and our rebellion opens a door for destruction from the devil!

So in considering the topic of "You're only as strong as your weakest link", I encourage you to examine your heart and life before God. How is your speech? Do you have any areas of depression and discouragement, anxieties and worry? How is the intake and outtake of the Word? Are you headstrong and prone to pride? Are you in any form of denial? Is God calling you to more prayer and fasting or a new venture in ministry? Do you need to get some accountability in your life? Have your hobbies become idols? How are your finances in regard to earnings, savings, investments, and tithing? Do you need to sharpen your gifts and skills, or get more education? What has the Holy Spirit been saying to you lately but you keep ignoring Him?

So what might be your weakest link that you need victory over, or more refining and increase in your life? It is not about being legalistic, but it is about being all that we can be in God, experiencing the fullness of the Spirit with meaning and purpose! So I encourage you to live your life in daily surrender and obedience to God and stay alert to the little things in your life!

Amen!!!

Do You Love Me?

John 21:15-17

This is the famous scripture where Jesus reinstated Peter. The night Jesus was betrayed, Peter denied Him three times. Now Jesus is asking Peter three times whether he loves Him. "Do you love Me more than these?" (John 21:15b NKJV). Jesus was implying to the other disciples when He said, "more than these." Matthew 26:33 (NIV) recorded that Peter had previously said, "Even if all fall away on account of You, I never will." Obviously Peter was full of pride before his fall. This serves as a reminder to all that none of us are above falling; we need to humbly rely on the Holy Spirit and His grace everyday.

In Jesus' three questions of "Do you love Me", He used two different words for love in the Greek language. In the first two requests of Jesus, He used the word "agape". Agape is the highest level of love. It is divine; it is God's kind of love as is seen in 1 Corinthians 13:4-7. It is selfless and people and things are second to God.

Peter's response was with the love word "phileo". Phileo is a brotherly kindness and friendship kind of love. So in Jesus' third request He also used the word phileo. At this request, Peter got upset. In Jesus using phileo it mirrored Peter's responses, and thus he was upset because Jesus was confronting his heart. According to Hebrews 4:12, God's Word will always discern the thoughts and intents of our hearts!

My friends, Jesus is to be more than a friend, though He is, more than a brother, though He is, and definitely more than an acquaintance. But our love for Him is to take preeminence in our lives (Colossians 1:18 and Luke 14:26). In other words, Jesus is to be the highest rank, order and power in our lives. He is to be superior to all!

In looking at the story of the rich young man in Mark 10:17-27, we see that our love towards God is more than being religious and keeping commandments. "Jesus looked at him and loved him. 'One thing you lack,' He said. 'Go sell everything you have and give to the poor, and you will have treasure in heaven. Then come, follow Me.' At this the man's face fell. He went away sad, because he had great wealth." (Mark 10:21-22 NIV). Actually, great wealth had him.

What is it that has you? What in place of God has all of your affection, energy, time, money and concerns? Are you regarding any sin in your heart? Many times when Jesus spoke, man's heart would be exposed. Jesus never sugar coated His Words. He would speak some very hard Words at times, especially when He spoke of our commitment to follow after Him. In Mark 4:16-17 (NIV) Jesus said, "Others, like seed sown on rocky places, hear the Word and at once receive it with joy. But since they have no root, they last only a short time. When trouble or persecution comes because of the Word, they quickly fall away." The Words of Jesus need to get rooted in us, not just tickling our ears with feel good messages. The more His Word gets rooted in us, the more we will grow and yield to His Lordship!

"This is my prayer: that your love may abound more and more in knowledge and depth of insight." (Philippians 1:9 NIV). That was Paul's prayer for the saints and it is my prayer for you as well as myself.

Always remember we love Him because He first loved us. It is out of His great love that He has called us and graced us with the privilege to serve Him!

Amen!!!

Night Vision

God tells us in Acts 2:17 that He will speak to us in dreams and visions.

Recently, I had a night vision in two parts. It began with myself and some other Christian brothers, out on the water fishing all day and we did not catch any fish. Then an old man came to the dock after fishing all day and his cooler was full of fish. In the second part of the vision I saw a man by the shore trying to catch a poisonous water moccasin. This man had experience at catching poisonous snakes and because he was so familiar with doing this he was careless. In his carelessness, his head was bent forward towards the snake and the snake extended in its strike and bit the man in the upper part of his back. It was a very deep bite too.

The Holy Spirit then gave me the interpretation to the vision. First of all, fishing and catching fish is a common reference in the Bible for a harvest of souls saved (Mark 1:17 and Matthew 13:47-50). You can toil all day trying to reach people for Christ, sometimes without any results. The old fisherman that caught fish is a picture of what Proverbs 11:30 teaches: "He who wins souls is wise." The old man knew the waters, he knew where to fish, how to fish and what bait to use. He was experienced! Many times we spin our wheels doing religious stuff without any life changing results. The old man is a picture of wisdom in action. Wisdom starts with prayer, praying for the condition of our hearts, and for the hearts of those we will reach out to with the Gospel. We want to yield to the power of the Holy Spirit, knowing what to say and when to say it, trusting in God's timing and leading. And we want to yield to faith and not doubt and fear. When we apply these wise foundational principles to our witnessing efforts, we will see greater results.

The second part of the vision is a picture of a Christian that has experience and knowledge in dealing with the devil, but in his pride he becomes careless and was injured severely. In 2 Corinthians 2:5-11, Paul is addressing the Corinthians about being obedient in everything and walking in total forgiveness towards others, in order that Satan would not outwit them, and thus being aware of his schemes. Satan has many tricks and deceptions to try to lure us into defeat. Christ has spoiled Satan's powers and made a public spectacle of him (Colossians 2:15). Therefore, Satan has to try to trick us into cooperating with him in order to defeat us in any way. So pride is one of the ways that he will use to try to destroy us. Scripture continuously warns against it, as in 1 Corinthians 10:12 and James chapter 4.

But many times, pride will gradually slip into our lives because we have become so familiar at doing life and ministry a certain way that we start to let down our guard. This is all the more reason to spend even more time on our knees and faces in prayer, relying on the Holy Spirit in every move of our lives!

There are several meanings to the snake biting the man in the upper part of his back. Firstly, a deep bite at the base of the neck affects the brain stem. All movement in our body comes from the brain. Satan wants to cause a disconnection between God and us by affecting our spiritual brain stem, which is prayer and yielding to the Holy Spirit. He wants to prevent us from thinking with the mind of Christ and having our minds renewed by the Word of God.

A serious injury in the upper part of your back will affect your posture. God wants us to stand firm in Him with our shoulders rolled back in a poise of confidence and boldness. When we are fearless in life and ministry, the devil fears us. So Satan wants to defect our spiritual posture in Christ.

The conclusion to all of this is to consistently pray without ceasing, yielding to the Holy Spirit, being confident and bold in Him, yet always walking in humility. The only way we can properly balance boldness and humility in our lives is by prayer. You can go to extremes into a ditch with either one. Always keep your guard up, not allowing yourself to become careless. "Knowledge puffs up, but love builds up." (1 Corinthians 8:1b NIV). And remember to seek God's wisdom in all ministry endeavors!

Amen!!!

But I Have Prayed For You!

Luke 22:31-32 NIV "Simon, Simon, Satan has asked to sift you as wheat. But I have prayed for you, Simon, that your faith may not fail. And when you have turned back, strengthen your brothers."

Jesus spoke these Words to Peter before he denied Jesus three times. This scripture should give every believer hope and encouragement.

Satan is always looking for legal grounds to sift someone. He is always seeking whom he may devour (1 Peter 5:8). We give Satan legal ground to sift us when we yield to sin, doubt, fear, and words of unbelief out of our mouths. As Proverbs 18:21 (NKJV) says, "Death and life are in the power of the tongue, and those who love it will eat its fruit." The preceding verses to 1 Peter 5:8 speak of humble submission and God opposing the proud. That is where Peter was prior to denying Jesus three times.

The real issue is not whether or not Satan can or will sift you, but the fact that Jesus prayed for Peter and He has prayed for us! Jesus prayed that Peter's faith would not fail.

Falling is not failing. Staying down and never getting back up is failure. When Jesus died on the cross for our sins, that represented His prayers for us. The cross is intercession and mediation between God and man. Jesus lives to intercede for us (Hebrews 7:25). His shed blood is a continual covenant of blessing and favor in God's kingdom. Therefore we always have hope for restoration when we have fallen. The grace of Jesus will always prevail on our behalf. Since our faith is based in His grace, we do not have to lose hope, no matter how hard we have fallen!

"And when you have turned back, strengthen your brothers." Jesus expects us to turn back. That expectation from Jesus gives us hope because He does not expect us to remain down and discouraged. This expectation also empowers us because we see in these Words that Jesus is also expressing faith and hope on His part toward us. Jesus believes in us! The empowering grace of the Holy Spirit will do everything possible to restore us and bring us back to fruitfulness. The opportunity to repent is a gift of God's grace (2 Timothy2:25-26).

No matter how we have fallen or how many times, always remember Jesus has called you to serve Him in a special and unique way. He does not turn away from His plans for your life (Romans 11:29 and Philippians 1:6). So hold on to that truth. You are not a washout. Keep believing and yielding. Press onward and upward in the name of Jesus. God's grace heals, restores, and empowers us. Your joy is connected in you connecting with His plan for you. Do not let the devil deceive you with accusations and condemnation. Always focus on God's awesome grace because Jesus has prayed for you!

Every time you receive communion, reflect on Jesus' Words from Luke 22:31-32. Remember that you are a partaker of His grace as you participate in the receiving of the bread and the wine (1 Corinthians 10:16-17). This is a special time to reflect and receive with faith and thanksgiving. It is also a time to be reinstated into fellowship with God and reinstated into His service. God is counting on you. Are you counting on God? And there are people counting on you to be reinstated, because each of us is a valuable asset to the kingdom of God!

So lift up your head and stand on the solid rock of Jesus and receive the abundant provision of His grace!

Amen!!!

Christ-Esteem

Everyone in life has some kind of personal view of himself or herself. Some have a positive self-esteem view, and some have a negative self-esteem. There are others that will have a mixture of the two. For those of us who are in Christ, we should not have any of those views, but rather a Christ-esteem. "That the communication of thy faith may become effectual by the acknowledging of every good thing which is in you in Christ Jesus." (Philemon 1:6 KJV). This was a prayer of Paul. According to 1 Corinthians 6:17, we are one with the Lord in spirit. We have become a new creation in Christ Jesus (2 Corinthians 5:17). In Christ we have been enriched in every way (1 Corinthians 1:5). We are full of goodness, complete in knowledge, and competent (Romans 15:14).

All of these grace-filled virtues are the new you in Jesus Christ. This is how we should see ourselves, based on what God says, not on our thoughts or emotions, which constantly change due to circumstances. What God has to say about us in Christ, is called our position in Christ. Many times our reality and experience in Christ is different from our position. But the more we focus on our position in Christ, confessing and acknowledging the truth of God's Word, the more we will actually experience these truths as well.

Just as Paul said in Philemon 1:6, as we focus on who we are in Christ, filled with all goodness, we will also communicate our faith more effectively, by word, and by life style. In 1 Corinthians 6:9-10, Paul listed some sins and then in verse 11 he said, "And this is what some of you were. But you were washed, you were sanctified, you were justified in the name of the Lord Jesus Christ and by the Spirit of our God." No sin from the past or present dictate who you are. But our faith in Jesus does dictate who we are!

"For He made Him who knew no sin to be sin for us, that we might become the righteousness of God in Him." (2 Corinthians 5:21 NKJV) At the cross an exchange took place.

Jesus took upon Himself our sin and we took upon ourselves His righteousness the day we were born-again. When we see ourselves as righteous and holy in Christ, we will live that way.

How we see ourselves in battle will also affect us in victory or defeat. When the twelve men went into Canaan to explore the land, ten came back with a negative report. They saw the great size and strength of the people and they said in Numbers 13:33 (NIV), "We seemed like grasshoppers in our own eyes, and we looked the same to them." If you see yourself negatively, as weak and fearful, then the devil will see you the same way. But if you know who you are in Christ, and what you have in Christ, being persuaded only by God's Word, then the devil will know and back down from you.

We are called to be mighty warriors of valor, full of confidence and authority in Christ. We were not called to be defeated! We were not called to be wimps! So whatever you are facing today see what God's Word has to say about it and press in to your position in Christ.

Christ-esteem! Christ-esteem! That is to be our focus in life!

Amen!!!

"The Word Of The Lord Came To Me"

Ezekiel 6:1

When you read the writings of the prophets you will see that sometimes God spoke to them in visions, and sometimes in an audible voice, but most of the time the Word came to them in their spirit. They heard the Holy Spirit speak just like we can today.

The Holy Spirit will put a Word or thought within you, usually when you are not thinking of the subject matter. When I practice being still and quiet before God, that is when I usually hear the Word of the Lord. When you are in an attitude of worship and prayer, God will speak. Ask Him to speak. Ask God what Word He wants you to deliver to someone. Think of yourself as a mailman, or a courier of the Holy Spirit.

Just today as I was in prayer, the Holy Spirit told me to call a certain person and say, "The Holy Spirit says to be still and know that I am God." The person responded by saying, "You are right on target, brother. I needed to hear that." I sent the same person a few exhortations by email recently, and he responded with the same reply again. It is encouraging to hear positive responses like that, but even if someone does not respond positively, we should not doubt the Holy Spirit. I would rather err on the side of faith and obedience, than doubt and disobedience.

I heard a Word for another person today and I called him too and delivered the message. Last week the Holy Spirit led me to call a man and read a scripture to him and pray with him. He too said it was a timely Word for him. There is an anointing that destroys yokes and removes burdens when we speak what the Holy Spirit gives us to deliver. It is not in the amount of words or whether it sounds all-religious. It is simply the Holy Spirit knowing the person's need, and you are available to be used. That is grace in action.

I have emailed some of the exhortations from this book

to various people at different times. Many have responded that the Word was timely for them in what they were going through. One person responded to my exhortation on tongues and said, "It came at a time when I had to minister a difficult Word to someone, and as I prayed more in tongues that week, it definitely helped." Praise God for His wisdom and timing!

A few months ago there was a woman that was in a valley of doubt and discouragement, and she had asked God to send someone with a Word for her. That afternoon God chose me to be the one. When I called her and delivered the Word, she was in shock, but she was also blessed and encouraged. Praise God!

Today I met a woman for the first time and she had just come from a Bible study on the love relationship with God. After the study she was struggling with the thermostat of her relationship with God. All of this unknown to me, God had me speak a Word from Song of Solomon 1:2 (NKJV), "Let him kiss me with the kisses of his mouth. For your love is better than wine." I said to her, "A Word of romance between a man and a woman is also being spoken to you from God. God immensely loves you!" Needless to say it blessed her. God is good!

I will also hear the Word of the Lord to pray for certain people about specific things in their life. As I pray for them in that specific area, sometimes I will also be prompted to send them a Word on the subject I am praying for them.

Ministry is joyous when you are hearing God and delivering the mail, especially when you see powerful fruit from it. I encourage everyone to spend time listening to the Holy Spirit, and respond to the prompts, even if it is one Word. Faith comes by hearing—the more we respond to what we are hearing, the more we will hear. It is exciting, fulfilling, meaningful, and powerful.

Let the Word of the Lord come to you. Do not quench Him, and do not hinder Him. Expect to hear and receive from the Spirit of the Lord!

Amen!!!

Persevere Under Trial

James 1:12 (NIV) "Blessed is the man who perseveres under trial."

Perseverance is patience and faith with endurance. Perseverance under trial is about patiently enduring during times of temptation and the testing of our faith.

Perseverance begins with a choice, a choice of refusing to give in and give up during difficult times. It is a choice of determination. I am determined to live my life for the glory of God, and I do not want to set a bad example of being a Christian. I choose the power of God's Spirit in my trials. I choose to listen to the Holy Spirit and to obey His leading. I choose to get on my face in prayer showing my humble dependence upon God, everyday and in every situation. I choose the living Word of God as my standard for life. I fervently choose the confidence and boldness that God gives me, and with authority I take my stand against the devil and all his lying spirits.

As we set our hearts and minds toward these kinds of choices, we prepare ourselves for victory instead of defeat. It is all about not being double-minded, as James 1:6-8 instructs us. The double-minded person wants to believe, but also looks at problems too closely, resulting in doubt. Doubt will pollute our faith, causing it to be ineffective, and we become unstable in all our ways.

"Blessed is the man." The person that chooses perseverance is empowered by God, because of his or her choices. It is that blessing of empowerment that will cause us to overcome and persevere. God's blessing is also divine favor in our trying situations. According to 1 Peter 5:6, God will exalt us as we humbly submit to Him. That exaltation is God's favor. Instead of the trial pulling us down and defeating us, God will turn it around for our good. We cannot go by what we are seeing and experiencing in the moment, but we have to see the big picture according to God's perspective. The big picture is that we are His covenant children, and He promises good things if we do not give in and give up, but continue to press onward and upward believing in God's goodness. Jesus said it perfectly to Martha in John 11:40 (NIV), "Did I not tell you that if you believe, you would see the glory of God?"

Spiritually speaking we have to train and discipline ourselves like a marathon runner. So with prayer, the Holy Spirit and the Word of God, we have to seek to grow and mature, becoming more like Jesus everyday. As Isaiah 40:31 (NKJV) says, "But those who wait on the Lord shall renew their strength, they shall mount up with wings like eagles, they shall run and not be weary, they shall walk and not faint." Here, waiting is perseverance. Waiting is not just sitting by doing nothing, but it is an action word of faith. In other words, we are seeking after God and trusting Him in all situations in life. Mounting up with wings like eagles is a picture of Holy Spirit strength, causing us to soar in life, overcoming the obstacles that come against us. The renewal of strength is new strength in God everyday. We do not live off of yesterday's strength, experiences or memories. Everyday is new in the power of the Spirit.

Lastly, another meaning of blessed is to be happy. In order to experience true happiness in life we need to persevere. Many are unhappy, depressed, discouraged, and in despair because they are not eagerly seeking to persevere. Instead, they take the easy road of giving up and giving in, thus reaping the negative consequences of fruitlessness.

So I encourage you to get some Holy Spirit determination and zeal and fight the good fight of faith and resist all double-mindedness!

Amen!!!

Do Justly, Love Mercy, And Walk Humbly With Your God

Micah 6:8 NJKV "And what does the Lord require of you, but to do justly, to love mercy, and to walk humbly with your God."

The prophet Micah declared what God expects of every one of His people. This Word was proclaimed in the Old Testament, but it also holds true for New Testament saints as well. The three items listed in the text define the values of a godly leader.

Before any of us can do justly and love mercy, we must first walk humbly with God. Without walking humbly with God, we may try to do good, but it will be a fruitless effort of a form of religion, with no power for change. In a summary of James 4:6-8, when we draw near to God, He draws near to us. Real humility is submitting ourselves to God. When we humble ourselves before God, He will give us grace. God's grace that He gives is an impartation of Himself in the Holy Spirit. The Holy Spirit gives us whatever we need in the moment, which includes the constant love and goodness of God, forgiveness and healing, strength and power, and wisdom.

Walking humbly with God is also a reflection of what Jesus said in John 15:5 NKJV, "I am the vine, you are the branches. He who abides in Me, and I in him, bears much fruit, for without Me you can do nothing." It also mirrors Philippians 4:13 NKJV, "I can do all things through Christ who strengthens me." In Christ we are a new creation (2 Corinthians 5:17). So we must always humbly reflect on who we are in Christ and what we have in Christ, and yield to that truth in a humble and submitted relationship with God.

Walking humbly with God is also about spending time with Him, talking to Him and Him talking to you. It is about seeking Him first, daily. As we spend time with God we will overflow with the abundance of His grace and power, like rivers of living water flowing in us and through us. Jesus mentioned this in John 7:37-39 in reference to the Holy Spirit in us.

Once we have established a relationship of walking humbly with God, then we will begin to love mercy and do justly. Mercy can be defined in two ways. One is love from God, where we do not receive the judgment we deserve. Another form of mercy is the compassion of God that reaches out to us. Compassion is deep sympathy. But from God's perspective, it is more than an emotion; it is emotion with action. We see a perfect example of this in Jesus in Matthew 9:35-36. As Jesus was moved with compassion, He taught the people, proclaimed the good news of the kingdom, and healed the sick. So we see that mercy leads to grace, which is God giving us what we do not deserve. We see in Hebrews 4:15-16 that because Jesus sympathizes with our weaknesses, we can approach God's throne of grace to receive mercy and find grace in our time of need.

Jesus said in Matthew 10:8 NKJV, "Freely you have received, freely give." So we are to be an extension of Jesus on earth reaching out to people with compassion in our hearts. It is important that we do not just do acts of mercy as a form of religion, but as the heartbeat of God within us. Notice that the verse says, "love mercy". We are not to grudgingly and grumbly do mercy, but love doing mercy. That will only come from the fire of our prayer closets. As we love mercy, we will notice the needs of the people around us, because we will be more sensitive to the Holy Spirit. In the context of mercy, also remember from James 2:13 NKJV, "Mercy triumphs over judgment."

Now to do justly means to do what is right in accordance with God's Word. It would be the same as the fruit of the Spirit of goodness. To do justly can also be described as acts of righteousness or walking in holiness. It is about integrity, doing what is right at all times, being honest and true to God, to self, and with the people we interact. To do justly is also mirrored in our speech, our work, ministry, relationships, private life, and public life.

As we see, this one verse of scripture is power packed with meaning, conviction, and responsibility. That is why this verse defines the values of a godly leader. We are called to be leaders. So let the truth of this verse be a plumb-line of godly standards in your life!

Amen!!!

Jesus—The Light Of Life

John 8:12 (NKJV) "I am the light of the world. He who follows Me shall not walk in darkness, but have the light of life."

John 1:4 (NKJV), "In Him was life, and the life was the light of men."

Jesus, as the light of the world, shines into our hearts to set us free from darkness and gives us divine direction and enlightenment.

Jesus is the light of God in the world and that light is in His life. As we yield to His life, receiving Him as our savior, receiving the gift of eternal life, then we have true light from God. This light from God gives us understanding of who God is and who we are in Him.

As Jesus said in John 8:12, when we follow Him we shall not walk in darkness. Isaiah 60:2 (NIV) says, "Darkness covers the earth and thick darkness is over the peoples, but the Lord rises upon you and His glory appears over you." There are the darkness of evil and satanic influence on the earth. There is the darkness of people yielding to a life of sin and selfishness. There is the darkness of fear. There is also the darkness of many kinds of natural disasters on earth. But the Lord rises upon us when we say "Yes!" to Him and His glory that appears over us is the light of heaven in Christ.

Isaiah 61:1 is a prophecy that is fulfilled in Christ. Jesus came to bring freedom for the captives and release from darkness for the prisoners. This is in reference to freedom from the power of sin and satanic strongholds. The power for the release of darkness is in believing the power of the Gospel (Romans 1:16), and then truly following after Jesus as a true disciple (John 8:31-32,36).

Colossians 1:12-14 clearly shows us that God rescues us from the kingdom of darkness and brings us into the kingdom of light in Jesus Christ. You are either in the kingdom of darkness or the kingdom of light. There is no in-between! Even if you consider yourself a good person but you reject Christ, then you are in the kingdom of darkness.

Here are some signs of darkness: you are confused about God and spiritual things; you have no peace or no direction; you do not know whether or not you will go to heaven when you die; you have no assurance about your eternity; you have hatred or unforgiveness towards someone; you fear death; you have a dark cloud of depression and despair, with no hope. Satan brings darkness and not knowing Jesus causes darkness.

But the good news of Jesus Christ opens the eyes of our hearts and turns us from the power of Satan to God, so that we may receive forgiveness of sins and enter into God's kingdom (Acts 26:18). This transformation takes place as we, by faith, receive Jesus as our Lord, yielding to the truth of the Gospel and confessing Him as Lord.

Here is an example of how you can enter into God's kingdom by praying a prayer like this: "Dear Lord Jesus, I believe you died for my sins and rose from the grave. I ask you to come into my life and forgive me. I'm sorry for my life of sin and I thank you for your free gift of salvation. I now confess you as Lord and ask you to fill me with your Holy Spirit. In Jesus' name. Amen."

And I say Amen to that!!!

David And Goliath

1 Samuel 17

Goliath stood over nine feet tall and he challenged the armies of Israel to send one man out to fight him, and whoever won the battle, the other army would be subject to them. At this challenge, Goliath came out everyday, morning and evening, and defied the armies of Israel. Goliath did this for forty days and the Israelites were dismayed and terrified.

Now David was just a boy who was sent by his father, Jesse, to deliver some food to the armies of Israel and to see how his brothers were doing, since they were serving in the army. While David was there he heard Goliath make his daily taunt, defying the armies of Israel. David's response was, "Who is this uncircumcised Philistine that he should defy the armies of the living God."

Even as a young person David understood the power of a covenant relationship with God, and that God was a covenant keeping God. Therefore, with this understanding of covenant, David knew that God would protect him and not Goliath. This is why David had such boldness and confidence in facing this giant.

We too can walk in such boldness and confidence as David for we are in covenant relationship with God, through the shed blood of Jesus Christ. That is why 2 Corinthians 1:20 (NKJV) says, "For all the promises of God in Him are Yes, and in Him Amen." Amen—meaning that is sure and complete in Jesus Christ.

So with such faith and confidence in God, David goes to Saul, the king of Israel, and says, "Let no one lose heart on account of this Philistine; your servant will go and fight him." Saul did not have much faith in David since he was a young boy and he was facing a giant that was experienced at fighting. David reassured him of how God protected him from the lion and the bear, and that God would protect him here as well. Not only did God protect him from the lion and the bear, but David pursued them in order to rescue the sheep.

David was fearless, a quality that we all need to walk in.

Saul tried to dress David with a coat of armor and a helmet, but David was not used to moving in it so he took it off. This is a reminder that we each have to serve God in our own unique gifts and talents that God has given us. We cannot serve like others; we have to be free and confident in this truth. Instead, David took five smooth stones and his sling to go fight Goliath, along with the name of the Lord.

As David and Goliath went to the battleground, Goliath taunted and cursed David and came towards him. It is at this point where many may retreat. Many talk a good talk but then they retreat in fear when the enemy does not retreat. When we resist the devil, always remember that we have to steadily resist in the faith, and keep proclaiming the Word of God. That is exactly what David did—he ran towards Goliath. Then he said, "I come against you in the name of the Lord Almighty, the God of the armies of Israel, whom you have defied. This day the Lord will hand you over to me, and I'll strike you down and cut off your head." As David ran towards him, he slung a stone at Goliath and it stuck in his forehead. Goliath fell down on the ground. David then ran towards him, took Goliath's sword and cut off his head.

When the Philistine army saw their champion beheaded, they turned and ran. At this time, the armies of Israel and Judah pursued them and the Philistine bodies were strewn dead all over the countryside. Just as the armies of Israel watched and then pursued the Philistines, so are there people watching us and waiting to see how we will respond in the course of spiritual battles. The faith and courage of others will feed off of us as we take a stand in the name of the Lord.

Always remember that the battle is the Lord's. God assures us victory if we will trust Him and follow His lead in all situations in life. Do not look at the size of the problem, but look at the size of God. All things must bow to His name. The devil is under His feet as well as our feet!

Amen!!!

Pride, Insecurity, And Rejection

Mark 9:2-37

This scripture in Mark's Gospel gives us a clear picture of what happens when we fall into issues of pride, insecurity, and rejection. Mark 9:2 tells us that Jesus took Peter, James and John with Him up a mountain alone. These three men may have felt a sense of pride when chosen to go with Jesus without the other disciples. The other nine disciples may have felt rejected and insecure because they were not chosen to go with Jesus. As we read on in the chapter we begin to see the scenario that played out.

Peter, James and John had an awesome experience on the mountaintop as they saw the glory of Jesus and heard the voice of the Father. Meanwhile, the other disciples were down in the valley dealing with the teachers of the law and a demoniac.

Mark 9:14-16 tells us that the disciples were arguing with the teachers of the law. The teachers were probably saying something like, "Who do you think you are trying to heal this boy and cast a demon out of him?" At this stage in the day, the nine disciples were probably feeling rejected and insecure, and at the same time full of pride, because they were being questioned about their power and authority to do such acts of ministry. All of the disciples previously had experience in healing and casting out demons, since Jesus had commissioned them to do such works of ministry.

Their pride, insecurity, and rejection led them into doubt, operating in the flesh, with no Holy Spirit power or faith. When the scenario was explained to Jesus, He responded with these Words from Mark 9:19 (NKJV), "O faithless generation, how long shall I be with you? How long shall I bear with you?" These Words were directed at the disciples. Therefore, we see that Jesus expected them to be able to heal and deliver. Jesus also expects the same of us today too. Jesus would probably have the same response today with most Christians.

As we see in the Gospel how Jesus healed and delivered the boy, we too are to operate in the same kind of faith and authority. Our faith is always in God's Word and the name of Jesus—not in past experiences. No matter how powerful a past experience was, we cannot assume that the same will happen again just by going through the motions. That is exactly what happened here: they went through the motions, but no faith and power this time. Pride, insecurity, and rejection are a deadly combination that weakens our faith.

In Mark 9:28 the disciples asked Jesus why they could not cast out the spirit. In Mark 9:29 (NKJV), Jesus said, "This kind can come out by nothing but prayer and fasting." Jesus' answer was not in reference to casting out the demon but getting rid of doubt. Luke 10:17 and Mark 16:17 clearly show us that casting out demons is by the name of Jesus, not spending more time in prayer and fasting. But, as we spend time in prayer and fasting we get more centered in the Word, and faith in His name, causing doubt to leave and faith to rise up within us. So the end result of more time in prayer and fasting can cause us to operate in more faith and power, but it is not a necessary antidote to demons, when we know the authority of Jesus' name.

In Mark 9:33-37, Jesus questioned His disciples about what they were arguing on the road. Their response was about who was the greatest among them. So we see that pride was at the core of each of these disciples. Jesus response in Mark 9:35 (NKJV), "If anyone desires to be first, he shall be last of all and servant of all." We all need to practice that more and more as a way to walk humbly before God and man.

Also in Mark 9:37 Jesus showed us how to really walk in love and humility by the way we treat children. An ounce of humility goes a long way in keeping us centered in real faith and power. I like to pray prostrate as a reflection to God of my humility towards Him.

In closing, remember that Satan will use pride, insecurity, rejection, and many other schemes as tools to trip us up in our walk of faith. Stay centered in who you are in Christ. Respond to every situation with the Word that gives faith and do not give into feelings of rejection and insecurity. Such negative feelings can become real strongholds that weaken you. But greater is He that is in you than he who is in the world!

Amen!!!

The Prodigal

Luke 15:11-32

This story is an illustration of our Father's love for us. It also gives us a clear picture of what grace looks like. The father in the story is a picture of God. The son in the story that wasted his inheritance is a picture of us all at some point in our lives. The older son is a picture of religion, with its legalism and judgment.

Many are already familiar with the story, if not read the scripture above. I am going to jump into the middle of the story after the son had wasted his inheritance with wild living and heads home to repent of his actions.

"So he got up and went to his father. But while he was still a long way off, his father saw him and was filled with compassion for him; he ran to his son, threw his arms around him and kissed him." (Luke 15:20 NIV).

Notice how the father saw him when he was a long way off. The father was diligently looking for him to return. God is also diligently looking for prodigals to return. Not only is God looking but also He is sending people to minister to the prodigals, and setting up providential circumstances to get their attention. Just like the father, God's compassion towards us all is based on His love for us; not our righteous actions. God is always running towards us, never away from us. He will also send people to hug you and kiss you as an embrace of his love.

As the son gave his confession of sin to his father, the father was more focused on celebrating his son's return. God is not moved by any prayers where we focus on our unworthiness. A prayer of submission and thanksgiving gets God's attention. Wallowing in feelings of unworthiness is religious and it has no powerful effects. Here again, it was the father's love that made all the difference. That is also where our focus needs to be: on our Father's love.

"But the father said to his servants, 'Quick! Bring the

best robe and put it on him. Put a ring on his finger and sandals on his feet. Bring the fattened calf and kill it. Let's have a feast and celebrate. For this son of mine was dead and is alive again; he was lost and is found.' So they began to celebrate." (Luke 15:22-24 NIV). This is what grace looks like, not focusing on the sin with judgment and rejection, but celebrating the return of a prodigal. The son did not have to do any kind of penance, as many of the religious would say is necessary. "In the same way, I tell you, there is rejoicing in the presence of the angels of God over one sinner who repents" (Luke 15:10 NIV). "He will rejoice over you with singing" (Zephaniah 3:17 NKJV).

God's people need to act just like God and the angels when a sinner repents. God wants us to celebrate His grace. The joy we experience in the celebration not only is liberating for the repentant sinner, but it is liberating for us as well.

In Luke 15:28-30, we see that the older brother was angry because of the celebration and refused to be a part of it. The older brother also focused on how good he was as an obedient son, and was quick to point out his brother's sin. All of this is a picture of dead, dry, legalistic, and judgmental religion, refusing to take part in a celebration of grace. Those who are stuck in this spirit of religion have no joy and are often angry at the mention of grace.

But the father pointed out once again in Luke 15:32 (NIV), "But we had to celebrate and be glad, because this brother of yours was dead and is alive again; he was lost and is found." That should sum it up for all of us, for we once were dead and are now alive, lost and now found.

Praise God for his wonderful grace! May we all know His love and grace in abundance, and rejoice with joy unspeakable!

Amen!!!

Power Packed Scriptures

Matthew Chapters 8 & 9

Matthew, chapters 8 and 9, are power packed with faith imparting scriptures. These are scriptures that deal mainly with healings, Jesus calming the storm, and Jesus calling sinners. Anyone that needs a booster shot of faith, I recommend reading and meditating on these two chapters.

Matthew chapter 8 begins with a man with leprosy asking Jesus if He was willing to heal him. "Jesus reached out His hand and touched the man. 'I am willing,' He said, 'Be clean!' Immediately he was cured of his leprosy." (Matthew 8:3 NIV).

Jesus is still willing to heal us today. So often we ask, "Is it Your will to heal me?" But God's Word clearly points out that it is His will to heal us. We need to go by what the Word says, and pursue our healing according to the Word as the final authority!

Matthew 8:5-13 is about the faith of the Centurion. The Centurion asked Jesus to heal his paralyzed servant. Jesus said, "I will go and heal him." But the Centurion replied to Jesus, "Just say the Word and my servant will be healed." Jesus said, "I have not found anyone in Israel with such great faith..... Go! It will be done just as you believed it would." And his servant was healed at that very hour.

What Jesus proclaimed as great faith was the Centurion believing in His spoken Word. The Bible is full of God's spoken Words. If we would believe like this Centurion, we too would see many healings and powerful results!

"He Himself took our infirmities and bore our sicknesses" (Matthew 8:17 NKJV). This verse was recorded as a result of Jesus healing many and was a fulfillment of prophecy in Isaiah 53:4. Matthew 8:17 and Isaiah 53:4 are the scriptures where the doctrine of healing provided in the atonement comes from. In other words, not only did Jesus carry our sins but He also carried our sickness and disease. This is also what Psalm 103:3 tells us. Many reject this doctrine because not all Christians are healed. I personally believe in this doctrine because it is what the Word says that counts, not people's experiences. Jesus bore the sins of the world, but not everyone receives forgiveness and gets saved. It comes down to us appropriating and receiving by faith what Jesus has provided, and fighting the good fight of faith standing on God's Word!

Matthew 8:23-27 tells us how Jesus rebuked the winds and the waves, calming the storm. Whatever storms we face in life, when Jesus is in the ship with us, we can have peace and no fear. Actually, we too can speak to the storms with authority having the same effects as Jesus, even literal storms.

Matthew 8:28-34 records how Jesus delivered the most violent demoniacs. No matter what kind of hold Satan has on someone, there is hope in Jesus!

In Matthew 9:1-8, Jesus was impressed with the faith of four friends who brought their paralytic friend to Him. Are you standing in the gap for sick friends, bringing them to Jesus, and bringing the faith filled Words of Jesus to them? And not only did Jesus heal the man but He forgave his sins, proving that He is God.

In Matthew 9:9-13 (NKJV), the religious spoke against Jesus for eating with sinners. Jesus response is seen in Matthew 9:12-13, "Those who are well have no need of a physician, but those who are sick. But go and learn what this means: I desire mercy and not sacrifice. For I did not come to call the righteous, but sinners to repentance." So if you are self-righteous and think you have nothing to repent, then Jesus serves no purpose for you!

In Matthew 9:17 (NIV) Jesus said, "Neither do men pour new wine into old wineskins." We cannot approach God in the New Testament the same way He was approached in the Old Testament. As Colossians 2:17(NIV) says, "These are a shadow of things that were to come; the reality, however is found in Christ." We now have a much better covenant in

Christ. Christ is better! Why go back to the old? You cannot combine the two covenants; it only leads to confusion and bondage.

In Matthew 9:20-22, a woman was healed for reaching out and touching the hem of Jesus' garment. Jesus turned and said, "Take heart, daughter, your faith has healed you." She was not healed just because Jesus had the power to heal. She drew out His power with her touch of faith. That is how we all need to approach healing: drawing it with faith in His power and grace.

In Matthew 9:25, Jesus had to put the noisy crowd, full of doubt and unbelief, outside the room before He brought a girl back to life. When ministering in healing and miracles, it is good at times not to be surrounded by those with doubt and unbelief. They can negatively change the atmosphere.

In Matthew 9:27-29 when Jesus had healed two blind men, he said, "According to your faith let it be to you." That is a central truth in everything that we receive from God.

In Matthew 9:32-33, a demon was driven out of a man that was mute. Then he could talk. Sometimes there are demons that are at the root of infirmities and afflictions. That is where the gift of discerning of spirits is necessary.

Lastly, in Matthew 9:35-38 we read about the compassion of Jesus that was the heartbeat of His ministry. We also read that the harvest is plentiful but the workers are few.

May we gain faith from these two power packed chapters in the Gospel of Matthew and may we go to the harvest field with the same compassion!

Amen!!!

Mary's Famous Words

Luke 1:38 (NKJV) "Behold the maidservant of the Lord! Let it be to me according to your word."

John 2:5 (NKJV) "His mother said to the servants, "Whatever He says to you, do it."

In Luke 1, this was Mary's response to the angel Gabriel when he told her she would bare the Messiah. In John 2, Mary said this to the servants prior to Jesus turning water into wine at the wedding in Cana of Galilee.

Mary's response to the angel Gabriel was a humble response. Gabriel was sent as a messenger from God; so actually, Mary's response was a humble response to God. She addressed herself as a maidservant of the Lord. Paul also said in Ephesians 4:1-2 (NKJV), "I, therefore, the prisoner of the Lord, beseech you to walk worthy of the calling with which you were called, with all lowliness and gentleness." It is in humbling ourselves before God that He exalts us. As we humble ourselves to His calling on our lives, we then, can walk it out with all power and might.

When Mary said, "Let it be according to your word", this was the wisest response anyone could give to God. Likewise, when the Holy Spirit speaks to us, may we all respond as Mary did! Remember it is better to err on the side of faith and obedience than on the side of doubt and disobedience. So often we try to squirm out of obeying God by saying, "I'm not sure if that was God speaking or not." If it was a Word that leads you in faith and love, and glorifies the name of Jesus, then run with it!

Also, in this context of Mary's response to Gabriel, God has spoken already and given us the Bible. We do not have to always hear some special Word from God as much as we need to respond to what has already been spoken. So as we read the Bible daily, we should respond as Mary did, by saying, "Let it be to me according to Your word." Sometimes we only respond to certain Words from the Bible, when we have an emotional response. But, remember we walk by faith and not by sight or feeling. So we can respond like Mary, even when there is no feeling or logic attached to it. I always say, "When we obey out of faith, then the positive feelings may come after."

Here's one for you, "What part of 'Go' don't you understand?" My good friend and mentor, Pastor Jim Brissey, wrote a book with that title. From the mandate of God's Word, we all are to go into the harvest field in one capacity or another. Even Paul the Apostle had feelings of fear and weakness (1 Corinthians 2:1-5).

So, when we respond like Mary as a servant, yielding to God's Word, then we will also have a response of joy as well, just as Mary sang a song of joy in Luke 1:46-55.

The next famous words of Mary was in John 2:5 (NKJV), "Whatever He says to you, do it." I believe Mary was prompted by the Holy Spirit to say that to the servants, because she knew something special and glorious was about to occur.

"Jesus said to them, 'Fill the water pots with water.' And they filled them to the brim. And He said to them, 'Draw some out now, and take it to the master of the feast.' And they took it." (John 2:7-8 NKJV). The water had turned to wine. Jesus' first miracle. But it would not have happened if the servants did not obey the Words of Jesus. You see, when we do our part in obeying, God does His part in making things happen. This is also true when we preach and teach the Word of God. Hearts are changed, and people get saved, only after we proclaimed the Word in obedience.

Also, just as the servants filled the water pots and drew water out, so are we to be filled with the Spirit, and draw from the Spirit, as rivers of living water (Ephesians 5:18 and John 7:37-39).

In conclusion, these words spoken by Mary are Spirit led, life changing, and full of faith. May we have the same wisdom as Mary in all of our responses to God!

Amen!!!

Do All In The Name Of The Lord Jesus

Colossians 3:17 "And whatever you do in word or deed, do all in the name of the Lord Jesus, giving thanks to God the Father through Him."

God the Father gave Jesus the name that is above every name (Philippians 2:9-11). We pray in Jesus' name (John 16:23-24). We do ministry in Jesus' name (John 14:12-14). We cast out demons in Jesus' name (Mark 16:17, Luke 10:17). We lay hands on the sick and see them recover in Jesus' name (Mark 16:18).

We do everything in Jesus' name because Jesus is the living Son of God that gave His life as a ransom for us. He gave us the power of attorney to use His name. As true followers of Jesus we bear His name and represent Him.

Every choice we make in life is either for the glory of His name or not for His glory. When we make choices in His name for His glory, it shows that we are committed to Him. We are committed as true followers when we do everything in Jesus' name. As a committed follower of Jesus, I choose to surrender my life and will to His care and control.

Jesus cares for us. He wants us to cast our cares and concerns upon Him. When I carry my concerns with fear and worry, then I am not choosing to do things in His name. Jesus wants us to yield all control of our lives to Him. Life is not about me being in control verses out of control, but it is about me living under His control. When I am not living under His control, then I am not choosing to do things in His name.

As Paul said in Philippians 2:9-11, every knee will bow and every tongue will confess that Jesus is Lord. Either now on earth or at the Day of Judgment, it is better to do it now with freedom and blessing, than later.

Jesus' name is above every name. His name is above sickness and disease. His name is above fear and doubt. His name is above depression and despair. His name is above poverty. His name is above every demonic stronghold. As we speak Jesus' name against these names in our lives, we can and will overcome and rise above them.

Every time you are tempted to smoke a cigarette, say, "In Jesus' name I don't need this and I cast down this addiction." And apply this same principle towards alcohol, pornography, food addictions, co-dependency, or any other kind of addictive behavior. And continue to do it steadfast in the faith of His name (1 Peter 5:9). We see an example of the power of His name in Acts 3:16 (NIV): "By faith in the name of Jesus, this man whom you see and know was made strong. It is Jesus' name and the faith that comes through Him that has given this complete healing to him, as you can all see."

When we make a conscious decision to do things in Jesus' name, it is based on our born-again love relationship that we have with Jesus. Because I love Him, I want to glorify His name in all I do. I also want to grow in my conscious awareness of my actions, knowing that I represent Him on the earth. I do not want to be a bad representation of His name, but a powerful one. May we all be more conscious of doing everything in His name, for His glory, and the glory of the Father! Also, may we all be more aware of the power in His name, thus walking in the victory that His name brings!

Amen!!!

Are You Increasing?

In 2 Thessalonians 1:3-4, Paul was affirming and encouraging the Church because their faith was growing more and more, and their love for each other was increasing. This growth was taking place in their lives in the midst of persecutions and trials that they were enduring. They were excelling in perseverance and faith. In a time where many would fall and falter, the Thessalonian church was increasing in faith, love, and perseverance. The key to their increase is found in 1 Thessalonians 1:6 (NIV), "You became imitators of us and of the Lord; in spite of severe suffering, you welcomed the message with the joy given by the Holy Spirit." They welcomed the Word of God with joy. That is what will bring increase into your life, regardless of what you are going through!

As a result of their increase in faith and love, they became a model to all believers in Macedonia and Achaia. Their faith in God had become known everywhere (1 Thessalonians 1:7-8). This had to be some powerful and radical faith in God in order for the news to spread everywhere of their changes in life. They had turned from their idols to God. This was not like many in church today, where they come to church on Sunday, but during the week they are still bound and lost.

If we are not increasing then we are becoming stagnant and decreasing. We are all called to grow and increase. It is a reflection of the pursuit of our heart. Do I want to be more like God? Do I want to reflect His image and power? I pray that, as you are reading this, the Holy Spirit is speaking and challenging you into action.

This theme is a common thread in scripture, which is why God is always speaking challenging Words, trying to get our attention. "May the Lord make your love increase and overflow for each other and for everyone else, just as ours does for you" (1 Thessalonians 3:12 NIV). "Finally, brother, we instructed you how to live in order to please God, as in fact you are living. Now we ask you and urge you in the Lord Jesus to do this more and more" (1 Thessalonians 4:1 NIV). Again, in 1 Thessalonians 4:10, they are urged by Paul to love more and more.

Here are some more challenging exhortations from God:

Jude 1:4 -contend for the faith.

Jude 1:20-21 -build yourselves up in prayer and keep yourself in God's love.

Philemon 1:21 -do even more than I ask.

Philemon 1:6 -communicate your faith even more effectively.

1 Thessalonians 2:2 -preach in spite of opposition.

1 Peter 1:13 -prepare your minds for action.

2 Peter 1:2 -grace and peace be multiplied in abundance.

2 Peter 1:5 -make every effort to add to your faith.

2 Peter 1:8 -possess these qualities in increasing measure.

2 Peter 1:10 -be more eager.

2 Peter 1:15 -make every effort.

I think you get the point.

So, are you increasing or decreasing? "Beloved, I pray that you may prosper in every way and that your body may keep well, even as I know your soul keeps well and prospers" (3 John 2 AMP).

Amen!!!

In All Your Getting, Get Understanding

Proverbs 16:16 (NIV) "How much better to get wisdom than gold, to choose understanding rather than silver."

Proverbs 16:22 (NIV) "Understanding is a fountain of life to those who have it."

Proverbs 20:5 (NKJV) "Counsel in the heart of man is like deep water, but a man of understanding will draw it out."

Proverbs 20:5 (NIV) "The purposes of a man's heart are deep waters, but a man of understanding draws them out."

Isaiah 55:8-9 (NKJV) "For My thoughts are not your thoughts, nor are your ways My ways," says the Lord. For as the heavens are higher than the earth, so are My ways higher than your ways, and My thoughts than your thoughts."

We cannot understand God and His ways with human reasoning and understanding. We need the divine impartation of the Holy Spirit in order to have real understanding. As the Son of Man, Jesus had that impartation of Holy Spirit understanding (Isaiah 11:2). How much more do we need that impartation of understanding?

When we study the Word of God, it is not just about receiving knowledge in our heads. We need revelation knowledge with wisdom and understanding. That is what Paul prayed for the churches in his letters to the Ephesians, Philippians, and Colossians. A good teacher will break the Word down for us and give us understanding with simplicity. That is what the Holy Spirit will do for us as we look to Him as our teacher.

As the Proverbs teach us, getting wisdom and understanding is much more valuable than any material riches in life. However, we have to choose it. It is a choice of pursuit. If we seek, we will find.

As Hebrews 3:7-19 teaches us, the Israelites had hardened their hearts during times of testing. Their hearts were always going astray and they had not known God's ways. Therefore, they could not enter God's rest. God does not want us to be ignorant of His ways. As we grow in understanding, we will prevent our hearts from hardening and going astray.

God wants us to understand His character of love and grace. He wants us to understand the power of the cross and all the wonderful workings of the Holy Spirit in our lives. He wants us to understand suffering and trials. It is important that we understand the deceitfulness of sin and the deceptive workings of Satan that will come against us. If we do not grow in understanding, then we remain ignorant and unwise by choice. Our understanding is limited at times, but God knows no such limitations. This is all the more reason to seek after God with all our hearts and continue to grow spiritually.

As Proverbs 20:5 teaches us, counsel and purpose abide within our hearts, but understanding draws it out. God has many purposes and plans for each of us. As we grow in understanding, we will draw out those purposes more and more. Others will also speak into our lives with Holy Spirit revelation and understanding thus helping us to pull from that fountain within. "A man's steps are directed by the Lord. How then can anyone understand his own way?" (Proverbs 20:24 NIV). God does not lead us year by year, or even day by day, but step by step. This is why we must live our lives in accordance to Proverbs 3:5-6 (NKJV): "Trust in the Lord with all your heart, and lean not to your own understanding; in all your ways acknowledge Him, and He will direct your paths."

Amen!!!

The Secret Things In Life

Deuteronomy 29:29 (NKJV) "The secret things belong to the Lord our God, but those things which are revealed belong to us and to our children forever, that we may do all the words of this law."

There are many secret things in life, that this side of heaven we will never know why things happen the way they do. But the things revealed are the revelation of God's Word given to man. There is enough revelation in the Bible to cause us to live powerfully and victoriously in life.

There can be a multitude of secret things that belong to the Lord. Why do children have to die at a young age? Why did that car accident happen, killing loved ones? Why am I going through this trial, Lord? Why do so many bad things happen to good people? Why was my child born with a disability? Why God? Why?

The real question to ask, is not "Why?", but "Who?". Who will help me with my trial and suffering? The answer is Jesus! Jesus is the "Who". He will walk with you and carry you in your sufferings and trials. Jesus is acquainted with grief, sorrows and suffering (Isaiah 53:3). He knows how to comfort, strengthen, and even bring meaning and good out of our griefs.

Now speaking of the things revealed, which is the Word of God, many of our questions in life will be answered, at least in a general way, just by a deeper knowledge of God's Word. We live in a fallen world and sin has brought chaos and suffering to the world. So even a child or a good and godly Christian is susceptible to pain and suffering that does not make sense. The sin of man can cause suffering in an indirect way, such as big industries taking shortcuts, and using toxic chemicals improperly, all for financial gain. The sin of a drunk driver can indirectly bring death to the innocent. As we all know and understand, there is death due to war and acts of terrorism.

Hosea 4:6 (NKJV) says "My people are destroyed for

lack of knowledge. Because you have rejected knowledge." It could be the knowledge of eating better and exercising. It could be the knowledge of being good stewards to our communities. And it is the knowledge of God's Word. As we hear, learn and understand what God is trying to teach us, a lot of unnecessary suffering can be prevented. Also, the knowledge of understanding that there is a real enemy against us, the devil. But as we gain insight on how to resist him and triumph over him, we again can prevent suffering.

2 Corinthians 1:3-7 teaches us that God will use our sufferings. The comfort we receive in the midst of them will turn out to comfort others in their suffering. Romans 8:28 reminds us that God will turn things out for the good for those who love Him and who are called according to His purpose. When we are going through pain and it does not make sense, remember God is there with you. He knows how to comfort the mourning and provide for those who are grieving (Isaiah 61:1-3).

It is also important to know that there are many things in life for which God will not give us answers. They are the secret things. But when God is quiet to your "Why?" questions, trust what He has given in the Bible. Do not allow yourself to become hardened and fallen away from God. Keep running to Him and His people. God is faithful and He will bring you through your most difficult pain and suffering. God is good all the time, and all the time God is good. We walk by faith, not by sight or feeling!

Amen!!!

Woman, You Are Loosed From Your Infirmity

Luke 13:10-17

Jesus was teaching in one of the synagogues on the Sabbath. There was a woman there who had a spirit of infirmity for eighteen years. She was bent over and could not raise herself up. But when Jesus saw her, He called her to Him and said to her, "Woman, you are loosed from your infirmity." And He laid His hands on her, and immediately she was made straight, and glorified God. It was a demonic spirit that had bound her for those eighteen years.

Many people who are bound with some kind of infirmity or incurable disease, are so because of a spirit that has afflicted them. As you read the Gospels, there are many occurrences where Jesus would cast out a spirit for someone's healing. According to Acts 10:38, Jesus healed those that were oppressed by the devil. To be oppressed means to be ruled or dominated. That can include your health, your mind, or a particular area of sin and weakness. Oppression can also be described as a spiritual stronghold. You can love God and serve God faithfully and still be bound in a certain area. But the good news is that Jesus has authority over Satan, and so do we in Jesus' name. Church, it is time that we wise up to the truth of demonic oppression, and to the truth of our authority in Jesus' name to minister healing and deliverance.

When Jesus saw the woman, He called her to Himself and spoke to her. We are the body of Christ here on earth, and we are His eyes and ears and mouth. Are we being sensitive to the Spirit in what we see, hear or say? The very fact that Jesus called her to Himself must have instantly brought hope to her. As a cripple for eighteen years, she must have felt shame and rejection, and now Jesus was calling her. Praise God for His call to all of us to be loosed and set free. Before Jesus laid His healing hands on her, He spoke to her with power and authority. Faith comes by hearing God's Word (Romans 10:17). So when Jesus said, "Woman you are loosed from your infirmity", that Word spoke faith into her to receive. When I minister healing to someone, I usually will speak the Word to them first before laying hands on them or saying any prayers.

We all need to hear and know that Jesus came, died and rose to life, in order to set the captives free, whatever we may be bound to. There is freedom in the name of Jesus, and as we follow Him and love Him, that healing and freedom will flow more and more. There is always hope in Jesus. Never give up! This woman was bound for eighteen years before her great day of God's visitation.

In this story it was the religious that got upset at Jesus for healing on the Sabbath. I love Jesus' response to them in Luke 13:15-16 (NKJV): "Hypocrite! Does not each one of you on the Sabbath loose his ox or donkey from the stall, and lead it away to water it? So ought not this woman, being a daughter of Abraham, whom Satan has bound—think of it— for eighteen years, be loosed from this bond on the Sabbath?"

Jesus constantly had to deal with the religious on the subject of the Sabbath. In Mark 2:27-28 (NKJV) Jesus said, "The Sabbath was made for man, and not man for the Sabbath. Therefore the Son of Man is also Lord of the Sabbath." Also in Matthew 12:12 (NKJV) Jesus said, "It is lawful to do good on the Sabbath."

I also like Jesus' response about the woman being a daughter of Abraham; therefore He ought to heal her. That speaks volumes on the subject of God's healing and blessing because of a covenant. God made a covenant with Abraham and Israel to show His kindness to them (Isaiah 54:10, 55:3). We have an even greater covenant with God in Jesus Christ. How much more can we expect to be healed and loosed from our infirmities?

After the healing and the Words Jesus had spoken, the religious were put to shame and humiliated. Jesus always spoke and ministered with such wisdom. May we speak and minister with wisdom, power and authority like Jesus did. In so doing, the religious and unbelieving around us will also be put to shame!

I pray this word of exhortation gives you hope and faith to be loosed of any infirmities in your life, and that you would be used as a conduit of God's power to loose others!

Amen!!!

A Man's Heart Reflects The Man

Proverbs 27:19 "As water reflects a face, so a man's heart reflects the man."

If you hang around someone long enough, you will see what is in his or her heart. Something that someone says will trigger what is in a person's heart, whether good or bad fruit. It cannot be concealed forever. According to Hebrews 4:12, the Word of God will also reveal what is in a man's heart. "...A tree is known by its fruit." (Matthew 12:33 NKJV). "... For out of the abundance of the heart the mouth speaks." (Matthew 12:34 NKJV).

It is important to know that there are two parts to a man's heart. They are the spirit and the soul. The Holy Spirit regenerates the spirit into Christ's image when you get saved, and out of our spirit we have a perfect connection with God. If you are not saved, your spirit is dead and lost in a sinful nature. The soul is our mind, will, and emotions. Our soul is not perfectly regenerated like our spirit is. Our soul-man needs to submit and be renewed according to the Word of God daily. It is out of the soul where strongholds may reside within us.

If we are walking in the Spirit daily and we do not have any spiritual strongholds, then what will come out of our hearts is the fruit of the Spirit. Our minds will also be renewed in the Word daily, dying to our own selfish wants, feelings, and thoughts. Our souls will always be in the renewal pattern till we go home to be with the Lord. Everyone has to constantly keep a check on the attitude of their hearts. It is all part of growth, being changed from glory to glory in Christ's image.

Now speaking of the overflow of the heart, speaking and reflecting the man, let us look at a few examples that tend to stand out. Rejection is one of those big ones that hits everyone at some point or another in life. But those that struggle with continual rejection usually were rejected by their parents as they grew up. Or, there might have been a series of rejections in their life by parents and spouses. Because of the rejection, a demonic spirit will enter their life and continually oppress them. Such a person will become hypersensitive to every word spoken and every action, feeding off of everything. Also, when some legitimate things occur that are upsetting, the rejected person turns them into unnecessary major crises.

Another area of the heart that shows its reflection is pride. Now pride will also be the downfall to a rejected person, because the rejected person does not want to admit their issues but wants to blame everyone else. Pride can be seen in self-righteous people who believe they never have any issues to look at in their lives. The prideful person is quick to point at the sins and issues of others, but never admits anything wrong in their life. Jesus spoke of that person in Matthew 7:3-6, having a beam in their eye, yet trying to remove a speck from their brother's eye. Pride will also be seen in the one that thinks he or she knows everything, and you cannot teach them anything. That person lacks a humble, teachable heart which is soft and flexible. Instead, their heart is hard and rigid. Even though a person might be doctrinally correct on the Bible, he or she may still exhibit pride with their know-it-all attitude. Also, pride opposes every form of grace. It is more about "look at me" instead of look at Jesus and what He has done for me and in me.

"For the Word of God is living and powerful, and sharper than any two-edged sword, piercing even to the division of soul and spirit, and of joints and marrow, and is a discerner of the thoughts and intents of the heart" Hebrews 4:12 (NKJV). As the Word is spoken to us, how we respond to it, is a reflection of our heart. Therefore, the Word is sharp enough to discern the attitude of the heart.

I pray this word is used to open the eyes of your heart. This is not a word to condemn anyone, but a word to reflect your heart like a face looking on water. In the grace of Jesus Christ there is hope and power for change and healing. We must first be willing to look at ourselves with all honesty, and then ask God to heal and deliver. He will powerfully set you free, but you may have to step through some painful thresholds in dealing with the issues of the heart. Ask a friend for some honest feedback. God will change you from glory to glory by the working of His Spirit!

Amen!!!

What Is The Lord's Will?

Ephesians 5:15-20

"What is the Lord's will for my life?" That is probably the most asked question among Christians. That question is even asked among non-Christians. For many the question implies reaching a particular place in life in a trade or ministry, or even a place of residence, or marital status. Those implications are part of God's will but they are not the whole pursuit of His will.

God's will for our lives comes in steps, day by day, and, most importantly, it comes out of a relationship with God. It is God's will that we get saved first and follow Him. In our pursuit of following Him, we become like Him. We will reflect His image as we spend time getting to know Him from the Word, prayer, and worship. Before we start to pursue some big picture of God's will, we must first take the baby steps of getting rooted and grounded in Him.

As we get to understand spiritual gifts and acts of service, try different acts of service. It is in trying different acts of service that you begin to see what you like to do, or what comes easily and with passion. Now every gift needs to be nurtured, and it is good to have mentors along the way. Also, over the course of life, God may choose to use you in different ways at different times. God may give you some more gifts that will sprout up over time with maturity.

We are all born with natural talents that God will use for His kingdom purposes, coupled with our spiritual gifts that come from spiritual birth. So if you have a talent that you want to pursue as your career, go for it. Some examples of natural talents would be mechanical, carpentry, plumbing, accounting, bookkeeping, music, art, administrative, sports, and many more. Paul was a tent maker by trade but a preacher and apostle by call. Some jobs that we have are not part of a divine call, but simply a way to make an income. But also remember that our jobs help us to grow in humility, submission, service, and selflessness. They help us grow because there will always be challenging situations that are stressful, especially in dealing with different personalities. All of this will drive us to seeking God more for strength and character growth.

I hear people say all the time, "I know God has a special plan for my life." My response to that is, do not live your life in tomorrow waiting for that something special to come. Live your life to the fullest today! Make the most of your opportunities today, and use your time wisely. Ask God what His will is for you today and be sensitive to yield to what comes your way. Go where God says to go and do what He says to do. Everyday will be different. Some will be trying. Others will be joyous. Take it all in stride. Whether you are in school, a trade, fulltime professional ministry, married, single, doing ministry at church as a volunteer, or a part time missionary in the summer, trust God in the moment knowing that you are in His will.

Also, remember that according to Ephesians 5:18 we are to continuously be filled with the Spirit. Yield to the fruit of the Spirit and the gifts of the Spirit daily. Yield to His timing, leading, and control. Let your heart abound and overflow with joy and gladness (Ephesians 5:19-20).

We will continue to grow and serve God, understanding what is His will, until we go home to be with Him. Life is a journey—one step at a time and one day at a time. God gave us the gifts of prayer and His Word to guide us every step of the way. There are no shortcuts in life. We must seek Him first and always, and trust Him. Then and only then, will the journey be filled with joy and power. There will be obstacles, valleys, and detours, but God will direct you!

Amen!!!

If You Believe, You Would See The Glory Of God

John 11:40

These are the Words Jesus spoke to Martha before the stone was rolled away from Lazarus' grave. In John 11:39 (NKJV), Martha was frantic and said to Jesus, "Lord, by this time there is a stench, for he has been dead for four days." Martha had expected Jesus to come and heal her brother Lazarus, but now that he was dead, she had lost hope of Jesus doing anything more. Jesus had greater plans than a healing. He was about to raise Lazarus from the grave after being dead four days.

Even when Jesus does not do what we had expected or when we had expected, do not lose hope. If you just believe, you will see the glory of God. God's plans and timing are much better than ours. We must not lose focus with the circumstances. God will be glorified in us and through us, as we trust Him. His glory that will be manifested is seen in the grace and power of the Holy Spirit at work in us.

The glory will definitely be the fruit of the Spirit flowing through us. When we choose to yield to all His fruit that is seen in Galatians 5:22-23, instead of frantic anxiety and fear, we will then walk in power and victory.

The glory will be seen as we yield to the gifts of the Spirit in operation in us and in the body of Christ. Here again as we trust Him, the answer we need may come in these gifts of grace.

The glory will be seen as we wait on His timing. "But those who wait on the Lord shall renew their strength; they shall mount up with wings like eagles, they shall run and not be weary, they shall walk and not faint" (Isaiah 40:31 NKJV). Waiting on the Lord is not sitting idle, doing nothing. Rather, it is seeking, trusting, believing, hoping, and doing. It is faith in action. This kind of faith is renewed in new Holy Spirit strength daily, causing us to rise above the circumstances, like an eagle soaring over the mountaintops.

The glory will be seen as we enter our prayer closets

consistently and persistently, shutting out the world and entering into that secret hiding place with God. It is here where we practice being still in His presence, and He will speak to us often.

The glory will be seen when we determine to praise God with a shout of triumph. It is when we choose not to let anything steal our joy, but instead we become more persistent with our joy, singing with jubilation!

The glory will be seen when we continue to renew our minds with the Word of God, thus being transformed into His image. The Word of God needs to be our plumb-line in life, setting our course for all decisions we make.

Also, the glory will be seen when we get our focus off of self. Life cannot be about me, myself, and I. It must be about God and others, even when it is difficult and painful.

Going back to the text in the Gospel of John 11, Jesus said in verse 25 (NKJV), "I am the resurrection and the life. He who believes in Me, though he may die, he shall live." Jesus even had authority over death. So, in Him, all things are possible. The good news however, is that in death there is glory too, when we know Jesus as our savior. And according to Isaiah 61:2-3, God will provide during a season of grieving. So in any and all circumstances in life we can expect to see God's glory if we will believe!

Amen!!!

Lord, Surely There Is A Stench!

John 11:39

When Jesus was about to raise Lazarus from the grave, Martha complained about the stench of odor coming from the grave. She did not want the stone rolled away, and thus would have missed out on the glorious resurrection of her brother, all because of a foul odor. So often we miss God's best because we are too focused on the stench of the problems, instead of God's power and glory.

Many times we are focused on the stench of our own sins. When we focus on the stench of our sins, we consider ourselves unworthy to receive anything good from God. When this happens, we are actually sabotaging ourselves. We fall into Satan's trap of listening to his accusations and condemning ourselves. There are three things to remember. First, if you are "in Christ", there is no condemnation placed upon you from God (Romans 8:1). Secondly, we are not to know anyone according to the flesh (2 Corinthians 5:16). That includes you. Thirdly, we are always to see ourselves like God sees us, in His grace, as the righteousness of God in Christ Jesus.

Another stench in people's lives is the stench of grumbling and complaining (1 Corinthians 10:10). This was listed as one of God's warnings from the example of Israel in the wilderness. Instead of complaining, we need to be thankful in all things in Christ Jesus (1 Thessalonians 5:18). Complaining makes things worse. Giving thanks makes things better. You cannot abound in joy if you are grumbling all the time. Your problems are not the fault of those around you. You have to choose joy and peace.

Then there is the stench of some form of demonic oppression. It could come in the form of rejection. It could come in the form of depression and despair, a dark heavy cloud. It could come in the form of hatefulness, envy, and bitterness. Or it could come in the form of fear. Regardless of which type of oppression may grip you, it becomes a foul stench that we focus on, thus preventing ourselves from receiving from God.

In John 11, the stone had to be rolled away before Lazarus was raised from the grave. It was in removing the stone that caused the foul odor of the corpse to vent out. In a very similar way people have the tendency to place a large stone, so to speak, over the stench of death in their lives. They live in denial, lock things away, never to be dealt with. They do not let anyone get too close, lest the stench be revealed.

Before any of us can experience true resurrection power in our lives, we must be willing to have the stone removed and let the stench out. Yes, there might be some shame and embarrassment at first, but God's love will overcome the shame. Just as Jesus said to Martha in John 11:40 (NKJV), "Did I not say to you that if you would believe you would see the glory of God?" It is all about us believing in God's love and power, and then we will receive His glory manifested before our very eyes.

There is not any sin, problem, or demon that God's power cannot handle. Are you willing to believe, roll away the stone, and let the stench come out? If so, you too will see His glorious power in your life!

Amen!!!

What Is The Proper Response To God's Call?

In 1 Kings 19:19-21, Elisha was plowing with twelve yoke of oxen when he received God's call to be a prophet. Upon receiving God's call, Elisha burned the plowing equipment, slaughtered the yoke of oxen, and then gave them to the people to eat. In so doing, Elisha was burning the bridge of what he knew how to do, and was not making it easy to return. After this, he followed Elijah as his attendant.

Sometimes we need to take drastic measures in responding to God's call, not making it easy for ourselves to go back to what is easy and familiar. Many will instantly go away to Bible College and Seminary, or begin training for the foreign mission field. I know a man that gave up his six-figure income and comfortable lifestyle to do the work of the ministry, reaching out to the homeless and those in prison. He has never looked back or regretted his decision.

Notice that Elisha followed Elijah. Elisha was mentored by Elijah, and he assisted him. It is important for pastors, evangelists, prophets, and teachers to be mentored. It is not just about getting head knowledge of the Bible, but it is seeing it lived out. That is what Jesus did with the twelve disciples. Paul trained others as well, such as Timothy and Silas. Two pastors mentored me for a couple of years, and I still learn from them. I started out as an associate pastor, and then became a pastor of a church, and I was released as an evangelist. Those few years of mentoring were priceless and rewarding.

We also see in Elisha following Elijah, that he humbled himself as a servant and was teachable. These are two unique qualities that are needed in responding to God's call. So often people will have Bible knowledge, or they may think, been there and done that, and pride gets in the way of their training. One thing that has to be learned by experience and observation is walking in the anointing of the Holy Spirit, learning to hear and follow the leading of the Holy Spirit.

Yielding to God's call is not like a nine to five, cushy

job. There is much sacrifice that comes with saying "yes" to God's call. But even with the sacrifices and difficulties there is an abundance of love, joy and fulfillment in saying yes. Paul proclaimed that his life was being poured out like a drink offering (Philippians 2:17). There are times when you give so much of yourself that you feel totally spent and exhausted. But God always refreshes you. Then there are the disciplines of prayer and fasting, and adequate time in the Word of God. Along with all that, you have to wisely balance your time to properly take care of your health and family relationships.

In Luke 9:62 (NKJV) Jesus said, "No one, having put his hand to the plow, and looking back, is fit for the kingdom of God." If you are plowing and look back, the plow will go crooked and off course. So we too are to keep our focus moving forward, in Christ. Our hearts are not to venture back on how things used to be without the demands of God's call. Life may have been easier before accepting God's call, but it was not as fulfilling, rewarding and life changing. And that means your life as well as the harvest of souls that you reach.

So what is the proper response to God's call? Jesus summed it up in Luke 9:23-25 (NKJV), "If anyone desires to come after Me, let him deny himself, and take up his cross daily, and follow Me. For whoever desires to save his life will lose it, but whoever loses his life for My sake will save it. For what profit is it to a man if he gains the whole world, and is himself destroyed or lost?"

The more we die, the more we live!
Amen!!!

God Prepares Us For Changes In Life

Isaiah 42:9 (NKJV) "And new things I declare; before they spring forth I tell you of them."

This was a Word of prophecy to Israel, but this same Word holds true for us today. Most of the time when God brings major changes into our lives, He prepares our hearts for the change. It could be how we have grown in our Bible studies and the fruit of the Spirit. It could be how we are learning to walk by faith and not by sight or feelings. It could be a prophetic Word spoken to us. Maybe a Rhema spoken from the Holy Spirit directly to our hearts. Or it could be God speaking to us by dreams and visions.

Now, even though God makes attempts at preparing us for changes in life, we have to respond. If we have become dull of hearing and are focused on self and problems in life, then we will miss what God is trying to say to us. It is all part of choosing to mature in our relationship with God. Changes can be good and fruitful when we are yielding to God, but they can make us miserable when we are not yielding to God. Which path shall you choose?

The Christian life consists of constant growth and maturity. With growth come changes and challenges. The only way to properly grow is of course to learn the Word of God in knowledge and application, living it out, and observing others living it out. This is also how we gain faith. The more of the Word you get in you, the more faith will come out of you. Our faith needs to be tried in order to come forth as true and genuine. If we are always fluctuating with our sight and feelings, then we are not walking by faith. Learning to walk in the fruit of the Spirit is another expression of our faith-walk. Yielding to joy instead of despair is faith. Yielding to peace instead of anxiety is faith. Yielding to love instead of anger is faith. So as we grow in the Word, faith, and the fruit of the Spirit, God is actually preparing us for some changes and challenges that will come into our lives.

God will send people to speak prophetically to you in order to prepare your heart for changes. Some may not even realize that they are being used by God to speak a prophetic Word to you, but regardless, God is faithful. If God can speak through a donkey (Numbers 22:28-30), then He can speak through any of us. As Paul said in 1 Thessalonians 5:20 (NKJV), "Do not despise prophecies." You cannot get any more clearer than that. We need to be open to receive from the Holy Spirit. It might not even be about major changes in your life, but simply about an attitude check, or a Word of inspiration for today's challenges.

Now just as God can speak to someone for a Word for you, He will also speak directly to you. That is called "Rhema" in the Greek. Actually God will speak directly to you more often than through others in prophecy. The real question is, are you listening, and are you preparing yourself to listen and receive. I am not talking about an audible voice from God, but the voice of the Holy Spirit speaking to our spirit. Most of the time the Holy Spirit speaks in a still and small voice, but some times the Word will resonate loudly in your spirit. The Holy Spirit uses the Word of God to speak to us, which is the most common way He speaks. The Holy Spirit speaks to me frequently in the area of ministering to people. He leads me where, when, how, and who. He also speaks to me through others in prophecy, but most of all, He speaks directly to me through the Word, prayer and worship.

Now God will speak to us in dreams and visions as well. God may speak this way to confirm what He has been saying already. Our spirit is more alert to receive in our sleep, since there are not any distractions from our environments. I encourage you to be open to dreams just as I urge you to be open to prophecy. Actually dreams are in the realm of the prophetic. God has given me direction for ministry through dreams and visions.

Now just as Isaiah prophesied, God will tell us of new things before they spring forth. So let us have ears to hear, eyes to see, and a heart to discern what the Spirit is saying

and we will be prepared for the changes in life!
Amen!!!

Determination

Matthew 7:7-11 (NKJV) **"Ask, and it will be given you; seek, and you will find; knock, and it will be opened to you. For everyone who asks receives, and he who seeks finds, and to him who knock it will be opened."**

Jesus continues on in verses 9-11 with a contrast between the goodness of an earthly father and that of our heavenly Father, who gives good things to those who ask Him. We see that our Father giving us good gifts is connected with our determination of asking, seeking, and knocking.

When we ask, it is a desire that is expressed. "You do not have because you do not ask. You ask and do not receive, because you ask amiss, that you may spend it on your pleasures" (James 4:2-3 NKJV). Jesus and James are telling us very clearly, "Ask". We do not need to be afraid to ask God for something. You will be amazed at how many times God will give you what you ask for, even little things.

Once when I went fishing with a friend, we put the boat in the river and floated down stream all day. I volunteered to go get the truck afterwards, which was miles up stream, and I said, "I'll be back shortly. God will provide a ride." My friend just chuckled, doubting my faith in God's goodness. Sure enough I got a ride right away and was back momentarily. My friend just shook his head in astonishment.

No matter how big or small the need is, God wants to be involved, if we would just ask. Now the flip side to what James said is that some do not receive because they ask with wrong motives. Check your motives when asking, focus on God's goodness, and do not have a "martyr's syndrome". A martyr's syndrome is when you purposely act pious by what you do not have, or by the difficulties you are experiencing.

Seeking is about searching. If our prayer life were more centered on searching after God's purpose, presence, and power, then we would receive in that realm. Many do not know God's purposes for his or her life. That is not God's fault. Many do not experience His presence and power consistently. Why is that? We will search our computers and TV guide, but we would not search after God!

Knocking is a word picture of determination. There are some things in life where God does not respond quickly because He wants to draw determination out of us. There's a perfect example of that in Matthew 15:22-28. A Canaanite woman approached Jesus to heal and deliver her daughter of demon possession. Jesus ignored her at first, and even appeared to be rude, but Jesus was drawing her faith out. Finally, Jesus praised her for her great faith and He healed her daughter. Are you knocking with determination for your healing? Are you determined in God to be set free from spiritual strongholds that have oppressed you all your life?

This three-step promise should drive us to our knees and further into the Word of God, with determination. This three-step approach towards God serves the purpose of drawing us closer to Him and being more dependent upon Him.

Matthew recorded in verse 11 that God gives good gifts to those who ask. Luke recorded in 11:13 that God gives the Holy Spirit to those who ask Him. The correlation between Matthew and Luke is that all of God's good gifts come through the Holy Spirit. So the more we get to know and understand the Holy Spirit, and the more we spend time with the Holy Spirit, the more we will actually experience God's goodness and power in our lives.

I pray that this word of exhortation encourages you to go further with God. Press in. God wants you to seek Him with determination, and thus you will receive the fruit of your determination!

Amen!!!

God Will Deliver

Isaiah 43:1-3 (NIV) **"But now, this is what the Lord says, He who created you, O Jacob, He who formed you, O Israel: 'Fear not, for I have redeemed you; I have summoned you by name; you are mine. When you pass through the waters, I will be with you; and when you pass through the rivers, they will not sweep over you. When you walk through the fire, you will not be burned; the flames will not set you ablaze. For I am the Lord, your God, the Holy One of Israel, your Savior.'"**

There are literally three examples in Israel's history where God did exactly that.

In Exodus 13:18, we see that God purposely led Israel around the desert road toward the Red Sea. Then in Exodus 14:4, we see that God hardened Pharaoh's heart, causing him to pursue Israel. But God would gain the glory.

There are times in our lives where it seems like we are facing a dead end, and the enemy is in hot pursuit against us. But if we will believe, and follow God's lead, He will be glorified.

In this story, the Egyptians were approaching the backside of Israel, with the Red Sea before them. The Israelites were crying unto God in fear and despair, but listen to Exodus 14:13-15 (NIV), "Moses answered the people, 'Do not be afraid. Stand firm and you will see the deliverance the Lord will bring you today. The Egyptians you see today you will never see again. The Lord will fight for you; you need only to be still.' Then the Lord said to Moses, 'Why are you crying out to Me? Tell the Israelites to move on.'" Then Moses raised his staff and stretched it out over the sea and God divided the water and Israel walked through the sea on dry ground. After Israel crossed over the Egyptians pursued them but God caused the sea to collapse on them.

The second story is found in Joshua chapter three.

God was moving Israel toward their invasion of Canaan, but there was one obstacle: the flooded waters of the Jordan River. The priests were to step into the river with the Ark of the Covenant. Once they stepped into the water, God kept the water back until everyone crossed over. The waters had to be raging down stream since they were flooded. I am sure the people were again gripped with fear. It took faith for the priests to take those first steps into the water. It was only then that God held back the waters. Sometimes we do not see God's deliverance until we are actually in the waters that appear to engulf us, but God will deliver. It is important to point out that the priests were to carry the Ark of Covenant into the river. The Ark of Covenant represents God's presence and glory. So as we face trials that could engulf us, focus upon, and yield to God's presence and glory, which is His Holy Spirit. God says, "I will never leave you, nor forsake you." This is especially true when we are facing our biggest trials in life. It is also important to note that this trial was before them, prior to approaching the Promised Land. Before we enter into God's best place for us, we will have to overcome some obstacles along the way!

The third story of God's deliverance is found in Daniel, chapter three. King Nebuchadnezzar had made a golden image ninety feet high and nine feet wide. Everyone was to bow down and worship the image whenever they heard the sound of music. Those who did not bow down and worship were to be thrown into a blazing furnace. There were three young Jewish men that refused to bow down and worship the golden image. They were given one last chance before the king to bow down, but they refused. Listen to their words before the king. "Shadrach, Meshach, and Abednego replied to the king, 'O Nebuchadnezzar, we do not need to defend ourselves before you in this matter. If we are thrown into the blazing furnace, the God we serve is able to save us from it, and He will rescue us from your hand, O king. But even if He does not, we want you to know, O king, that we will not serve your gods or worship the image of gold you have set up.'" (Daniel 3:16-18 NIV). The king was furious at their response and he ordered the furnace to be turned up seven times hotter than usual. Sometimes before we experience God's deliverance, the fiery trial gets heated up even more. The fiery furnace was so hot that the soldiers throwing them in were burned to death. After being thrown into the furnace, the king observed four men walking in the fire. They were unbound and unharmed. The fourth man was the Lord. The fire had not harmed their bodies, nor was their hair singed, their robes were not scorched, and there was no smell of fire on them. To God be the glory! Many times the greatest deliverance comes as we go through the fiery trial.

As you and I face trials in life, some things to remember from these three stories are these. Fear not, stand firm, and rest in God's provision. Move forward at His lead, and quit crying. Go in His presence and glory. Do not behold the raging waters and fiery furnace, but behold Him. The battle is the Lord's. No matter how trying the trial is, do not bow down to the enemy, but only bow before God. And God will bring you through the trial unharmed, unsinged, and no smell of fire, because He is always the fourth man walking with you through it all!

Amen!!!

Safety Of Abiding In The Presence Of God

Psalm 91

Psalm 91 is a Psalm of God's protection. But sometimes we do not see the protection as the Psalm describes. Some things that happen in life are a mystery as to why they happened. What many do not realize though, is that there are actions on our part mentioned in Psalm 91.

There are several actions on our part mentioned in Psalm 91:1-2 (NKJV). "He who dwells in the secret place of the Most High, shall abide under the shadow of the Almighty. I will say of the Lord, 'He is my refuge and my fortress; my God, in Him I will trust.'" The dwelling and abiding that are mentioned are about us yielding to God and having a close relationship with Him, just like Jesus said in John 15:5. Dwelling in the secret place is about entering into the place where God abides, which is in our spirit by the Holy Spirit. As we get still, pray and listen, our inner man becomes that secret hiding place that Psalms 31:20 and 32:7 mention. It is within that glorious presence of God that we experience protection, not only from physical harm, but also in the realm of oppression to our souls as well.

Another action that Psalm 91:2 mentions is that of our confession. What are you saying daily? Are you confessing that God is your refuge and fortress? There is power and faith expressed in our words. Both God and Satan operate from our words that we speak. If we speak words of doubt, fear, and depression, the devil and demons will use them against us. Those negative confessions become an open door for satanic attacks.

Psalm 91:2 also says, "My God, in Him I will trust." Is the Lord your God? "The Lord is good, a stronghold in the day of trouble; and He knows those who trust in Him." (Nahum 1:7 NKJV). There's no deceiving God. He knows what's in your heart. He knows whether you trust Him or not!

Psalm 91 continues in verses 5-6 (NKJV), "His truth

shall be your shield and buckler. You shall not be afraid of the terror by night, nor of the arrow that flies by day, nor of the pestilence that walks in darkness, nor of the destruction that lays waste at noonday." Paul said the same thing in Ephesians 6:16, taking up the shield of faith, extinguishing the flaming arrows of the evil one. It is God's Word in our hearts and minds that brings faith as a shield, and thus causing us not to be afraid. We also have to choose not to give into fear, not going by what our natural eyes see, but what our spiritual eyes see. We must resist the spirit of fear in Jesus' name and with God's Word. Then we will experience God's protection.

Psalm 91:9 (NKJV) emphasizes our rewarded actions again by saying, "Because you have made the Lord, who is my refuge, even the Most High, your dwelling place." As a result thereof, God sends His angels to minister to us as heirs of salvation (Hebrews 1:14 and Psalm 91:11-12).

Psalm 91:13 mentions us treading upon the lion and serpent. Jesus also said something similar in Luke 10:19. In the Psalm, it could be a literal lion and serpent, but in correlation with Luke's writing, it is speaking of the devil and demons. Peter even said that the devil is like a roaring lion (1 Peter 5:8). Here again action on our part is needed, as we are to walk in God's authority throughout life.

In Psalm 91:14-15 (NKJV), God says, "Because he has set his love upon Me, therefore I will deliver him; I will set him on high, because he has known My name. He shall call upon Me, and I will answer him." Our actions here are our love towards God. Our love is seen in our prayers and worship, seeking God first, living according to His Word, and yielding to His call in service. Another action is knowing His name. Knowing His name speaks of an intimate relationship with God, knowing the covenant blessings in His name, and the authority of His name. The last action is that we are consistently calling upon Him. That is what God wants us to do. Jeremiah 33:3 reminds us of that truth as well. The more we call upon God, the more we are expressing our dependence upon Him, and the more He will respond.

The final blessing is seen in Psalm 91:15-16 (NKJV), "I will be with him in trouble; I will deliver him and honor him. With long life I will satisfy him, and show him My salvation." This entire chapter speaks of the safety that we have in abiding in God's presence. It is not because of how righteous we are, but because God is full of love, goodness, power, and authority. And as a result of God's salvation, we respond with the actions mentioned in this chapter!

Amen!!!

Receive The Promise Of The Spirit Through Faith

Galatians 3:14

This scripture speaks to us in two ways. It speaks of the coming of the Spirit into us as believers in Jesus Christ. Secondly, whatever the Spirit promises us, comes through faith. Receiving the promised Holy Spirit comes through faith, and receiving the promises of the Spirit come through faith.

The prophets spoke of the Holy Spirit's coming. In Acts chapter two, we read of the Holy Spirit coming on the Jewish believers, and Acts chapter eight, He came upon the Samaritans, and Acts chapter 10, He came upon Gentile believers. Joel prophesied 2:28 (NKJV), "And it shall come to pass afterward that I will pour out My Spirit on all flesh; your sons and daughters shall prophesy." In Acts 11:16 Peter remembered what the Lord had said, "John baptized with water, but you will be baptized with the Holy Spirit." In Acts 2:36-38, on hearing the Gospel of Jesus Christ, the people were cut to heart, and said, "What shall we do?" Peter replied, "Repent and be baptized, every one of you, in the name of Jesus Christ for the forgiveness of sins. And you shall receive the gift of the Holy Spirit." This promise is for all, who will receive the promised Holy Spirit.

The promises of the Spirit that come by faith are justification and righteousness. To be justified means to be made righteous, just as if you never sinned. "God will credit righteousness for us who believe in Him who raised Jesus our Lord from the dead. He was delivered over to death for our sins and was raised to life for our justification." (Romans 4:24-25 NIV). "This righteousness from God comes through faith in Jesus Christ to all who believe." (Romans 3:22 NIV). "Now the just shall live by faith." (Hebrews 10:38 NKJV). "The righteousness of God is revealed from faith to faith." (Romans 1:17 NKJV).

This promise of justification and righteousness is a

promise from the Spirit for all who believe in Jesus Christ. We continue to see the fruit of justification as we walk by faith. Always remember, it is faith in God's grace, as Romans 4:16 points out, and it is never faith in our faith, as if we work it up in and of ourselves.

Along with receiving justification by faith from the Spirit, all of the Spirit's promises come by faith. "And since we have the same spirit of faith, according to what is written, 'I believed and therefore I spoke', we also believe and therefore speak." (2 Corinthians 4:13 NKJV). We see that whatever we believe, we speak according to what is written. So one aspect of receiving from the Spirit by faith is to continue to speak forth the promises. Since faith comes by hearing (Romans 10:17), we should also hear ourselves speaking the Word, building ourselves up in the Lord.

Now speaking of receiving from the Spirit by faith, this includes Rhema spoken to you about God's plans and purposes in your life. In 1 Timothy 1:18-19, Paul instructs Timothy to hold onto the prophecies spoken over him, so that he may fight the good fight of faith. If we reject prophetic utterances, then it may have an adverse affect to our faith. Continue to tap into what the Spirit is saying to you and receive it by faith, and with a good conscience.

"Does God give you His Spirit and work miracles among you because you observe the law, or because you believe what you heard?" (Galatians 3:5 NIV). This was the precursor question leading up to Galatians 3:14. All the glorious and powerful things that God does in our lives are not based on our human efforts to be good, but on believing in God's grace, and receiving by faith!

Amen!!!

Drawing From The Wells Of Salvation

Isaiah 12:3 (NKJV) Therefore with joy you will draw from the wells of salvation.

This chapter of scripture is a picture of Israel when Jesus is reigning as their Lord. The messages in this chapter apply to Christians today, since Jesus is already reigning as our Lord. In John 4:14, Jesus said that the water He gives is a well of water springing up into everlasting life. So wells of salvation are a picture of the many different blessings that come from our source of salvation—Jesus Christ Himself.

When you draw water from a well, you lower a bucket into the well to draw the water, or you prime it through a pump. So there is an action that takes place to draw the water out. The same is true in drawing from the wells of salvation. There is an action on our part in drawing out the many different blessings.

As Isaiah prophesied, we use joy to draw from the wells of salvation. In Ephesians 5:18-20 and Colossians 3:16 Paul tells us that the Spirit-filled life is expressed in having a heart of gratitude, singing psalms, hymns and spiritual songs. So we see in these scriptures that the well of power and anointing in the Holy Spirit is drawn by joy.

In Acts 16:22-34, with joy Paul and Silas drew from the well of deliverance and a special anointed time to get a family saved. Paul and Silas were not delivered from the beating and flogging, but they were delivered from the "woe is me" attitude of grumbling. They chose joy in the face of pain and suffering. God will do supernatural things in our lives when we choose joy. It is a choice to yield to joy, just like it is a choice to yield to anger, fear, and grumbling.

For the joy that was set before Him, Jesus endured the scorn, shame, and pain of the cross (Hebrews 12:2). With joy, Jesus drew from the well of strength to endure through a painful trial. In James 1:2-8 we are instructed to draw with joy from the wells of perseverance, wisdom, maturity, stability, not lacking anything. Those are some big demands on our faith, but with joy, all things are possible.

Joy is that one fruit of the Spirit that is connected to everything we do. If we resist joy, it is almost impossible to accurately draw from all the different wells of salvation. Yes, you could draw from these different wells of salvation without joy, but it would be hindered and lacking.

As I had mentioned, drawing water from a well could come from priming a pump. Sometimes that is exactly what we are doing when we begin to praise and worship God. There are times when you may be down, oppressed, and obsessed, but as you allow yourself to enter into that joyful atmosphere of praise and worship, you will begin to draw from the different wells of salvation. These different wells could be a healing, deliverance from demonic activity, and a prophetic Word spoken that brings divine direction and encouragement into your life. It could be you receiving a blessing from any of the spiritual gifts in operation at a church service, or you being used in any of the spiritual gifts.

The wells of salvation are connected to the main source of life and blessing, called the rivers of living water (John 7:38). Jesus told us that if we thirst and drink from this source, living water will flow from within us. Not only does joy come from this living water called the Holy Spirit, but also joy becomes the source within to continually draw all other blessings into our lives as a constant overflow of the grace and power of the Holy Spirit.

So if you want to live the blessed life, draw from the wells of salvation with joy!

Amen!!!

Cannot Be Shaken

Psalm 21:7 (NIV) **"For the king trusts in the Lord; through the unfailing love of the Most High he will not be shaken."**

Psalm 125:1-2 (NIV) **"Those who trust in the Lord are like Mount Zion, which cannot be shaken but endures forever. As the mountains surround Jerusalem, so the Lord surrounds His people both now and forevermore."**

Psalm 119:165 (NKJV) **"Great peace have those who love your law, and nothing causes them to stumble."**

There are several key ingredients that keep us from being shaken. The first ingredient is trusting in the Lord. To trust in the Lord is placing all your faith and hope in God and His promises. You are not moved or shaken by the storms in life. Storms will come our way, but we are not to let them dictate our faith. Just as Jesus taught us in Matthew 7:24-27, the one who stands in the storm, is the one who built his house on the rock. The rock represents the one who is a doer of the Word and not a hearer only.

Not only are we to trust in the Lord, but also it is His love that is the foundation of our trust. "How great is the love the Father has lavished on us, that we should be called children of God." (1 John 3:1 NIV). "And so we know and rely on the love God has for us." (1 John 4:16 NIV). We can rely and trust in God's love when we know His love. To know His love speaks of an intimate relationship with Him. "There is no fear in love; but perfect love casts out fear, because fear involves torment." (1 John 4:18 NKJV).

When we have an unshakable trust in God's love, then we will not be afraid of any storms that come our way. We do not doubt God's love and provision through the Gospel of Jesus Christ and the Holy Spirit. In His perfect love, we cast down all fear that would try to shake us. Fear torments us to doubt and despair, laying aside all hope. But our trust in God's love causes us to be strong to the core, immovable and unshakable.

We can have constant endurance and stability because God surrounds us forevermore. He surrounds us with His love, power, authority, and great and precious promises. Therefore we cannot be shaken!

Another key ingredient that prevents us from being shaken is our love for God's Word. Love for His Word brings the fruit of divine peace into our lives. God's peace is the inner strength and resolve that sustains us in every trial we face. To love God's Word is to delight in it, memorize it, meditate on it, confess it, and to pattern your life according to it.

So are you trusting in God's unfailing love? Have you allowed His perfect love to reign in you, resisting all fear? Have you developed a love for His Word? Are you yielding to His peace within you?

I pray that your life is unshakable and immovable to the glory of God!

Amen!!!

The Storm Before The Calm

Luke 4:35 (NIV) "Be quiet" Jesus said sternly, "Come out of him." Then the demon threw the man down before them all and came out without injuring him.

Mark 9:25-27 (NIV) "You deaf and mute spirit." He said, "I command you, come out of him and never enter him again." The spirit shrieked, convulsed him violently and came out. The boy looked so much like a corpse that many said, "He's dead." But Jesus took him by the hand and lifted him to his feet, and he stood up.

Many times things look worse before they get better. The devil will try to make things worse one last time before a healing or deliverance takes place, or before we receive an answer to our prayers.

The devil knows he has to respond to the authority of God's Word and Jesus' name, but if he can get us to into the realm of doubt and fear, then we just became double-minded. As James 1:7-8 tells us, a double-minded man is unable to receive anything from the Lord and is unstable in all he does. But we see from Jesus' examples that He was never moved by the last moment antics of the devil. He remained full of confidence in His own authority. God wants us to get to that place as well, on the receiving end of God's power, and in ministering in God's power.

We can nullify a prophetic Word spoken to us or Rhema coming from our prayer and study time, if we begin to doubt and murmur because the heat of affliction is being turned up. As Paul said to Timothy several different times, "Stir up and fan into flames those prophetic words spoken over you, and fight the good fight of faith." Paul was urging Timothy because he had a tendency to be timid. We have to be full of courage and faith, not being moved by what we see or experience. When we know who we are in Christ and what we have in Christ, and Whose we are, then we can stand strong unwavering in our trials. Sometimes God may give you a Word for someone and they may not receive it. Do not let that discourage you, doubting what God has spoken to you.

As another example, you may have experienced a healing when someone prayed over you, then days later some sickness symptoms return. Many at this time will say, "Well I guess I didn't really get healed." They end up remaining sick by speaking of what they see or feel. It is at this time that you have to fight with the Word of God. We can speak with power and authority to our bodies and against the sickness. I know of a woman that had MS and was in a wheelchair, who got completely healed. But it was only after she continued to speak God's Word over herself, resisting the enemy. She would experience breakthrough in her healing and then some setbacks, but she persisted in her faith. Now the battle is over and she is sharing her story of God's healing power. She experienced many storms before the calm, but she did not give up.

The same type of thing can happen with having a financial breakthrough. First, we need to settle the issue of giving tithes and offerings. It needs to be revelation to us by the Holy Spirit, and then not wavering when times are tight. Secondly, we need to give with gratitude and faith, expecting God to bring breakthrough in our finances. Thirdly, speak the Word of God over your financial seed, expecting a harvest. Now even if there are setbacks and storms, do not give in to doubt and fear, but fight the good fight of faith.

Another example is when you are seeking after God with all your heart and trying to serve God, and pandemonium breaks loose in your home and family. The devil will try to use anyone, or any circumstance to stir up division in the home. It could be a misunderstood word that was spoken. It could even be a family member that is tired and stressed, with low blood sugar. At these times we do not retaliate against one another, but we press in more in our prayer closets, resist that spirit of division in Jesus' name, and yield to the fruit of the Spirit.

In Mark 5:22-24 and Mark 5:35-43, there was a little girl that was sick and Jesus was called upon to come and heal her. Jesus began to go to their house, but was delayed. During the delay, the girl died. Jesus said, "Don't be afraid; just believe." When Jesus got there he raised the girl back to life. Many times our situations in life look very dark and dismal, but we need to hear the Words of Jesus as well, "Don't be afraid; just believe." And the Words Jesus spoke to Martha in John 11:40 (NKJV) before Lazarus was raised from the grave, "Did I not say to you that if you would believe you would see the glory of God?"

I have given you many different scenarios in life that we all face. The main thing to remember, according to Ephesians 6:12-13 (NKJV) is, "For we do not wrestle against flesh and blood, but against principalities, against powers, against the rulers of the darkness of this age, against spiritual hosts of wickedness in the heavenly places. Therefore take up the whole armor of God, that you may be able to withstand in the evil day." The victories are ours to receive, but we must walk by faith and not give into doubt and fear!

Amen!!!

In Christ Dwells All The Fullness Of The Godhead

Colossians 2:9-10 (NKJV) "For in Him dwells all the fullness of the Godhead bodily; and you are complete in Him, who is the head of all principality and power."

Jesus is the heir of all things, who made the worlds (Hebrews 1:2-3). He is the brightness of God's glory and the express image of His person. He upholds all things by the Word of His power. "All things were created by Him and for Him. He is before all things, and in Him all things hold together" (Colossians 1:16-17 NIV).

So many people get confused about the deity of Jesus Christ. There are even cults that believe in God, but they have completely missed it when it comes to Jesus being the fullness of the Godhead. It is really quite simple. The Father and Son are one; you cannot have one without the other. When you read the scriptures that I quoted, you either accept them by faith, or you try to use human reasoning to explain them. Human reasoning will always lead you astray from the foundational principles of Jesus Christ. In Colossians 2:6-8, Paul explains that we are to be rooted and grounded in Christ, being strengthened in our faith. Make sure no one takes you captive through hollow and deceptive philosophy. For it is in Christ that we are complete. It is not anything in place of Christ, or in adding to Christ. But it is in Christ and Christ alone that we are saved and complete.

Apart from Jesus Christ in our lives, we are empty, without meaning and purpose. Nothing can fill the God vacuum in us but Christ alone. Man will try to fill their lives with many different things, but it is meaningless and void, like chasing the wind.

Jesus is head over all power and authority in life. Every position of royalty, presidents, thrones, angels, demons, and mankind must bow to His Sovereign authority. We can bow out of a humble loving relationship with Him, or we can bow at the Day of Judgment.

To be complete in Christ means you have accepted Him into your life as Lord and Savior. He changes you into His image, being Christ like. You now have a new nature and spirit.

The completeness means you are full of Him in your spirit. As we yield to that fullness in Christ, our mind, will, emotions, and body will be blessed as well. So, to be complete means there is nothing lacking. Yes, we all have to grow in the grace and knowledge of Jesus Christ, but there is no lack in the source of our new lives, in Christ.

To be complete in the fullness of Jesus Christ is our position in Him. Our experiences might not be lining up with our position in Him, but the more we focus on that position, and acknowledge our fullness in Him, the more it becomes a reality. So never lose sight that Christ is the fullness of the Godhead, and that He upholds all things by the Word of His power. There is no lack in Him!

Amen!!!

Vision, Imagination, And Revelation

Proverbs 29:18 (KJV) "Where there is no vision, the people perish."

Proverbs 29:18 (NKJV) "Where there is no revelation, the people cast off restraint."

Ephesians 3:20 (NIV) "Now to Him who is able to do immeasurably more than all we ask or imagine, according to His power that is at work within us."

Ephesians 3:20 (NKJV) "Now to Him who is able to do exceedingly abundantly above all that we ask or think, according to the power that works in us."

Proverb 23:7 (NKJV) "For as he thinks in his heart, so is he."

We become what we think. We think in accordance to what we see. And we pray, how we think. Do you pray with Holy Spirit enlightened vision and revelation, or do you pray with limited vision? Is your vision carnal, coming from your senses and environment, and thus causing doubt and fear? Or is your vision full of imagination coming from the Word of God, thus not limiting God?

"Yes, again and again they tempted God, and limited the Holy One of Israel." (Psalm 78:41 NKJV). We limit God when we doubt Him at His Word. We limit God when we are not willing to believe big. As Ephesians 3:20 tells us, God is able to do awesome and powerful works, but it is in correlation to our imagination. Imagination is spiritual sight by the Holy Spirit.

To cast off restraint, as Proverbs 29:18 says, is to abandon yourself to your own sinful ways. When we lack vision and revelation from the Word of God then there is the tendency to do just that. It is important for our growth that we are always putting ourselves in position to learn. Our minds and imagination need to be constantly stretched.

We need to see ourselves doing great works for the

Kingdom. I see myself preaching to large crowds, and thousands of souls getting saved. I see myself healing the sick and raising the dead. I see myself ministering to the brokenhearted and oppressed and seeing them set free. I see myself imparting the fire of God into others, through my preaching and teaching, and praying over them. I see thousands of souls being ministered to through this book. I am not full of myself; I am just full of God with vision and imagination. As I envision it and pray it, I know God will do even more than I ask, according to the power that is at work within me. Praise God!

So how about you? How do you see yourself? How do you see God? Are you ready to receive your healing? Are you ready to answer God's call? Are you ready to let God begin stretching your imagination? Are you ready to start taking God at His Word and quit doubting Him?

As you imagine God's greatness at work within you, it stirs up a Holy Spirit excitement and expectation. We are in the last of the last days and it is time that we get serious with our Christian lives! Let the shackles fall off. Let the blindness be removed. Let the prison walls come crashing down. And let us move forward doing the Father's work with power and might, with no restrictions by our stinking thinking!

Amen!!!

What Are You Pregnant With?

Matthew 13:31-32 (NKJV) "The kingdom of heaven is like a mustard seed, which a man took and sowed in his field, which indeed is the least of all the seeds; but when it is grown it is greater than the herbs and becomes a tree, so that the birds of the air come and nest in its branches."

Matthew 17:20 (NIV) "If you have faith as small as a mustard seed, you can say to this mountain, 'Move from here to there' and it will move. Nothing will be impossible for you."

1 Peter 1:23 (NKJV) "Having been born again, not of corruptible seed but incorruptible, through the Word of God which lives and abides forever."

Galatians 4:19 (NKJV) "My little children, for whom I labor in birth again until Christ is formed in you."

We see in 1 Peter 1:23 and Mark 4:1-20, that the Word of God is the seed that impregnates us, and it is an incorruptible seed. Whatever you are pregnant with, you will bear fruit of its kind. By the Word of God, we become pregnant with the life of God, and the kingdom of God. Even though there may not be any evidence of that kingdom for some time, eventually a little sapling will burst through. As Jesus said in Mark 4:28 (NKJV), "For the earth yields crops by itself; first the blade, then the head, after that the full grain in the head." A pregnant woman may not show evidence of being pregnant for months, but the seed has definitely been planted. As Jesus mentioned, the kingdom of God being like a mustard seed planted which grows into a huge tree, so it is in our hearts and lives. We do not want to discount small or slow beginnings.

Your faith may also appear to be small as a mustard seed, but that seed of faith in Christ and His Word will produce significant results. Your life in Christ is significant! Regardless of a difficult upbringing as a child, disabilities, or no education, you are pregnant with value and significance. And all things are possible for Christ's followers impregnated with His faith-filled Word.

The huge tree produced from the small mustard seed is a picture of our abiding life in Christ (John 15:5). As we abide in the life of the vine, which is germinated from the seed, we will bear much fruit. God will exalt you and raise you up to do great things in His name and in His Spirit.

In Galatians 4:19, Paul was pregnant with the labor pains of intercession for the Galatians. He was laboring to see the Galatians filled with the fullness of Christ in their lives. So we see that Paul was pregnant with divine purpose in ministering Christ. We also see in Colossians 1:28-29, that Paul labored and struggled with all energy to present everyone man-perfect in Christ. What divine purposes are you pregnant with? Has God put a burden on your heart for prayer, proclamation, teaching, helps, or leadership? Are you pregnant with a burden for a specific group of people or nation? Are you pregnant with the Word of God, faith, and vision?

As you bring forth the birth of any aspect of the kingdom of God, know that there will be labor pains. But just as a mother rejoices with the birth of her baby, you too will be full of joy, regardless of the labor pains!

Amen!!!

Husbands And Fathers

Ephesians 5:25-26 (NKJV) "Husbands, love your wives, just as Christ also loved the church and gave Himself for her, that He might sanctify and cleanse her with the washing of water by the Word."

Ephesians 6:4 (NKJV) "And you, fathers, do not provoke your children to wrath, but bring them up in the training and admonition of the Lord."

Colossians 3:19 (NIV) "Husbands, love your wives and do not be harsh with them."

Colossians 3:21 (NIV) "Fathers, do not embitter your children, or they will become discouraged."

1 Peter 3:7 (NKJV) "Husbands, likewise, dwell with them with understanding, giving honor to the wife, as to the weaker vessel, and as being heirs together of the grace of life, that your prayers may not be hindered."

Men, God is calling us to be godly leaders in our homes. Our wives and children want us, and need us to be godly leaders in our homes. You can give without loving, but you cannot love without giving. Giving is the heartbeat of serving. Lust wants to consume for self, but love is giving. It is time we quit making lame excuses and take the helm of the ship.

We need to start by walking in humility and not pride. It is out of pride that we do not do anything, because we do not want our family to see our weaknesses, or lack of knowledge and abilities as a godly leader. We all fall short. That is where humility comes in, depending on God's grace, and help of the Holy Spirit.

As we walk in humility and not pride, we need to stop being controlling. Communicate love through your grace-filled actions. As godly leaders in our homes, we need to build up and not tear down. Do not talk badly about your wife in public, and never use her as the punch line in any joke. Our wives and children are not to be our verbal punching bags! Spend quality time with your wife and children, having a cup of coffee together, going for walks or bike rides. Do not talk about problems all the time. Set boundaries for that, such as the family dinner table, and when you are trying to have some fun and quality time together. Do fun things with your kids that they want to do.

Husbands, read the Bible with your wife and children, and pray with them. When praying together, pray prayers that build them up. If your wife knows the Bible better than you, do not let that keep you from learning it and teaching it. Do not use that as an excuse; our wives want us to lead them. Pray with your wife about family decisions and direction, about financial matters, and discipline of the children. If there are disagreements, do not take them as rejection. It simply means that the two of you see things differently. Let that be an opportune time for searching for truth from the Word of God, prayer, and gentle communication. "A soft answer turns away wrath, but a harsh word stirs up anger" (Proverbs 15:1 NKJV). "Bear with each other and forgive whatever grievances you may have against one another. Forgive as the Lord forgave you" (Colossians 3:13 NIV). To bear with, means to put up with and deal with graciously. Men, many times this is where we blow it, because of our egos.

As 1 Peter 3:7 points out, husbands are to dwell with their wives with understanding and consideration. We all know that there are many differences between the male and female, but for some reason we seem to think that our wives should think, feel, and act just like us. Well, wake up and smell the coffee, because that's not going to happen. Men, the more we have a better understanding of our wives, the better we will get along. We also need to consider their needs and help them with their fears and insecurities, instead of belittling them. We need to practice the art of honoring our wives. We are partners together in this grace-filled life. Therefore, when we practice these principles, our prayers will not be hindered.

Fathers, remember that your children are a heritage and reward from the Lord (Psalm 127:3). We need to teach our children about God, raising them up in the ways of God. Set the example for your children on how to know God and walk in the Spirit. Let them see you and hear you pray consistently. Let your children see you loving their mother and grandmother. Let it be your ambition to have your home be a place of refuge and healing, instead of dysfunction and abuse. It is time to stop the cycle of abuse, addiction and dysfunction. We do not need more medicine for our kids; we need miracles! We need divine intervention, and it starts with us, men! We need to stop being absentee fathers, and show some interest in our children. Pray over your kids. Prophesy over them. And bless them.

For some, all of this may be a hard task in life. It may be hard if you never had a godly father to set the example for you. You also may have been abused and experienced all kinds of dysfunction in your home while growing up. Maybe your father was an absentee father. With all that being said, know that in Christ, things can turn around for you and in you. Your Heavenly Father will heal your broken heart, and He will lead you and teach you by His Spirit.

"Freely you have received, freely give" (Matthew 10:8 NKJV). Keep on receiving from the river of life, the Holy Spirit, and keep on giving from the Holy Spirit. Continue to have grace for yourself. Let yourself be healed, and be a vessel of healing to your family. God can and will restore your family. Do not ever give up. Believe!

Amen!!!

Wine And Strong Drink

1 Corinthians 10:31 (NKJV) "Therefore, whether you eat or drink, or whatever you do, do all to the glory of God."

Ephesians 5:18 (NKJV) "And do not be drunk with wine, in which is dissipation; but be filled with the Spirit."

Dissipation is to waste or squander, and it is indulging in pleasure to the point of harming oneself. When we choose to drink alcohol, many times we are wasting away our relationship with God, and misusing valuable time to serve Him. And we harm the name of Christianity. Drunkenness should not be part of a Christian's life. "Walk in the Spirit, and you shall not fulfill the lust of the flesh." (Galatians 5:16 NKJV).

There are too many in the Church that confess Jesus as their Lord, and still drink alcohol in excess. When you play with fire, you will get burned. Anyone that drinks alcohol will always have the tendency to drink too much. You may think that you want to honor God and not drink too much, but there is the natural lust of the flesh that will want more once that door has been opened.

I speak from experience on this matter. When I got saved thirty years ago, God set me free from drug and alcohol use. I went many years walking in freedom. Over a course of time I had some new friends that would have a few social drinks, and I began to have a few social drinks as well. For the most part, I was under control, but I opened that old familiar door of a lust to the flesh. Over a course of time, 1-2 drinks turned into 3-4, then 5-6. I also noticed my Christian friends were having that same tendency to drink too much. So finally the Holy Spirit spoke to me, "You are not to drink at all, due to your weakness in the flesh, and my call on your life." That settled that! I have obeyed ever since. Praise God!

Let us look at what the Word of God has to say on the subject. "Wine is a mocker, strong drink is a brawler, and whoever is led astray by it is not wise" (Proverbs 20:1 NKJV). Under the influence of alcohol you will mock God and people, and there is the tendency to fight. For most, it is verbal, not physical, but either way, it does not glorify God. God says here that it is foolish to be led astray by the use of alcohol. "Harlotry, wine, and new wine enslave the heart" (Hosea 4:11 NKJV). I remember when I started drinking again, even though it was not much, I had lost the fire of God in me. I do not ever want to lose that again. Alcohol will enslave you and take away your heart after God. Proverbs 23:29-35 gives us a clear picture of the effects of alcohol usage: "Who has woe, sorrow, and wounds without cause, the one that is deceived by the appeal of alcohol?"

In Isaiah 5:11-12, 28:7-8, and Amos 6:6-7, these two prophets rebuked Israel for their excessive use of alcohol. They had become more focused on indulging themselves, than on the work of God's kingdom. How about you? If you are drinking, take a good look at your life, and examine the effects alcohol has had on you, your family, and your relationship with God. Just because you go to church and do religious things does not mean that God is pleased with your actions. It is time we wake up to the call of God, and let the fire of His Spirit burn all the chaff out of our lives.

Now Romans 14:21 speaks loudly to those who say they are free to drink. If your freedom causes a weaker brother to stumble, then you sinned. How about your children that see you drink all the time? How will that affect them as they get older and are faced with the choice to drink or not?

In 1 Timothy 3:3 and 3:8 and Titus 2:3, Paul gives instruction by the Holy Spirit that leaders in the Church are not to indulge in drinking too much wine. But the real question is, "Who sets the limits?" It should be the Holy Spirit. If you are going to serve God in a leadership role, you are better off purging alcohol out of your life altogether. In

Luke 1:15 we see that the Holy Spirit set the limits for John the Baptist. He was not to have any wine or strong drink in his life. It makes perfect sense. If we are going to represent God, hear Him, and communicate His truth in power, then we should avoid the use of alcohol.

In closing, reflect on the 120 that were filled with the Spirit on the Day of Pentecost. Some thought they were drunk with wine since there was so much joy and rejoicing under the power of the Holy Spirit. Why get artificial and temporal joy from alcohol, which leads to sadness and despair, when you can have the real and eternal joy in the Holy Spirit? Which shall you choose? I choose life and life more abundantly!

Amen!!!

Neither Do I Condemn You; Go And Sin No More

John 8:11

These are the Words that Jesus spoke to the woman caught in the act of adultery, found in John 8:3-12.

Sometimes Christians have the mindset that "I'm just a sinner saved by grace". With that mindset we accept our sins and say, "I'm just human." But that thinking needs to be tweaked. Now in Christ we have become saints, which means holy ones. We are the righteousness of God in Christ Jesus. So when we get saved, God calls us and empowers us to live a life free from the shackles of sin.

"For the grace of God that brings salvation has appeared to all men, teaching us that, denying ungodliness and worldly lust, we should live soberly, righteously, and godly in the present age." (Titus 2:11-12 NKJV). We cheapen grace when we make excuses for sin. Grace was never meant to be a license to still sin freely. Paul wrote about this in Romans 6:1-4 (NKJV), "Shall we continue to sin that grace may abound? Certainly not! How shall we who died to sin live any longer in it?" Paul continued on saying, "Even so we also should walk in newness of life." The grace of God not only forgives, but it makes us new and empowered in Christ, to live a holy and godly life.

I think some who continue in a life of sin, have not been truly saved. Yes, they believe in God, but they may not have committed their hearts to Him. "Repent therefore and be converted, that your sins may be blotted out" (Acts 3:19 NKJV). Repentance is an act of turning away from sin and turning towards God. What direction is your life going in? "Repentance and remission of sins should be preached in His name to all nations." (Luke 24:47 NKJV). I think too often we leave the repentance part out of the equation. John the Baptist said in Luke 3:8 (NIV), "Produce fruit in keeping with repentance."

"Most assuredly, I say to you, whoever commits sin is a slave to sin." (John 8:34 NKJV). Jesus is not speaking of an occasional fall that may happen to anyone. He is speaking of consistent and habitual sin. "If you abide in My Word, you are my disciples indeed. And you shall know the truth, and the truth shall make you free." (John 8:31-32 NKJV). Here, Jesus is talking about being set free from the power of sin that enslaves. God wants us to be true disciples of Him, abiding in His Word. That is what real Christianity looks like. We are to be free, and free indeed.

Basically what Jesus was saying to the adulteress woman is, "I love you, I forgive you, I do not condemn you, but you must choose to follow Me and abide in My Word, so you don't fall back into your sin." That is what God has to say to all of us. God offers freedom to us all through the power of the Gospel, the Holy Spirit, and the Word of God.

What shall you choose? Will you be a true disciple of Jesus Christ? Or will you bear the name of "Christian" and continue to be a slave to sin? Will you cheapen grace or will you embrace true grace that empowers?

May we all produce fruit in keeping with repentance. For God has rescued us from darkness into light, and from the power of Satan to God (Acts 26:17-18). Go and sin no more!

Amen!!!

Servant Of All

Mark 10:42-45 (NKJV) "You know that those who are considered rulers over the Gentiles lord it over them, and their great ones exercise authority over them. Yet it shall not be so among you: but whoever desires to become great among you shall be your servant. And whoever of you desires to be first shall be slave of all. For even the Son of Man did not come to be served, but to serve, and to give His life a ransom for many."

In Philippians 2:7-8, we see that Jesus humbled Himself and became obedient to the point of death, even the death of the cross. He made Himself of no reputation, taking the form of a bondservant. "He now showed them the full extent of His love." John 13:1 (NIV). These are the Words recorded prior to Jesus washing the feet of His disciples.

A bondservant is one that was a slave and is now free, but he or she chooses to still be a servant. Jesus chose to be a bondservant for us, making Himself of no reputation. Yes, Jesus was known for all the great things He had done, but they were all done with a servant's heart. Whatever works we do in the kingdom, should not be about a reputation of our name, but to serve others.

What are your desires? If you desire to be first in anything, it is to be done by being a slave to all. Those are some pretty strong Words from our Lord. The only way that can come about is through humble submission to our Lord. It does not come natural. It is supernatural. Even those that minister on a platform in front of everyone, their success is based on an attitude of love and service, to honor God. If we get full of ourselves, God can remove an anointing just as quickly as He gave it. Actually, the anointing will always be connected with compassion towards people.

"And Stephen, full of faith and power, did great wonders and signs among the people." (Acts 6:8 NKJV). Stephen was one of the seven chosen to be deacons in the church in Jerusalem. They were chosen to serve the widows, so the Apostles could focus on prayer and the ministry of the Word. I believe it was because Stephen had such a servant's heart that He could be used in ministering miracles among the people. As his heart was moved with compassion towards the people, while serving them, his prayers brought forth miraculous signs.

"You wicked and lazy servant" (Matthew 25:26 NKJV). These are the Words our Lord spoke to the man that buried his talent out of fear, and did nothing to bring increase. Do you choose to do nothing out of fear? If so, you have made the focus about you instead of the glory of God. Experiencing any kind of increase in our lives begins with a servant's heart.

We see in John 13 that Jesus showed the full extent of His love by washing His disciples' feet. Have you ever washed someone's feet? Are you willing to bow down in service toward someone? The lower we go, the higher God will raise us. As Jesus humbled Himself unto death on a cross, God gave Him a name that is above all names (Philippians 2:7-11). It is never about getting a name for ourselves, but you see the principle.

"Whoever can be trusted with very little can also be trusted with much." (Luke 16:10 NIV). "From everyone who has been given much, much will be demanded; and from the one who has been entrusted with much, much more will be asked." (Luke 12:48 NIV). These two scriptures are the spoken Words of Jesus. The core of these verses is about being a servant and trustworthy. Once we show ourselves faithful in the little things, more will be given. This truth applies in our homes, in our places of business, in the Church, and kingdom work.

May we not hear the Words "You wicked and lazy servant." But may we hear the Words of Jesus in Matthew 25:21 (NKJV), "Well done, good and faithful servant. Enter into the joy of your Lord." To the glory of God!

Amen!!!

Joshua's Orders

Joshua Chapter 1

In Joshua chapter one, God spoke to Joshua to succeed Moses in leading Israel into the promised land of Canaan. The Words that God spoke to Joshua were Words of courage to believe God and not to give into fear. This chapter of scripture will give courage to all who are called by God to lead. We are all called to be leaders in one capacity or another, so it is wise for all to take heed to this exhortation.

In Joshua 1:2 (NIV), God says, "Get ready." It is important that we all live our lives ready to succeed. Readiness speaks of the attitude of our hearts in seeking after God, listening, expecting, and a willingness to obey. "If you are willing and obedient, you shall eat the good of the land; but if you refuse and rebel, you shall be devoured by the sword." (Isaiah 1:19-20 NKJV). When you have a willing heart, it exudes with anticipation and expectation for God to do great things with you, in you, and through you.

"Every place that the sole of your foot will tread upon I have given you." (Joshua 1:3 NKJV). This verse speaks of God's people appropriating what is already rightfully theirs. As they went and tread upon the land, it was theirs to possess. The same is true for us today in regard to forgiveness, healing, prosperity and provision. As we believe and receive, we are to move forward possessing what God's Word says is ours. That is exactly what Jesus said in Mark 11:24 (NKJV), "Therefore I say to you, whatever things you ask when you pray; believe that you receive them, and you will have them." You have to see it by faith and divine revelation first. That is what will spur us on to action.

"No one will be able to stand up against you all the days of your life. As I was with Moses, so I will be with you; I will never leave you nor forsake you." (Joshua 1:5 NIV). Joshua was Moses' assistant. He saw how God was with Moses. What a Word of encouragement to know that, in all the ways you saw God with your mentor, so will He be with you. Paul also exhorts all Christians the same way in Romans 8:31-34 (NKJV), "What then shall we say to these things? If God is for us, who can be against us? He who did not spare His own Son, but delivered Him up for us all, how shall He not with Him also freely give us all things? Who shall bring a charge against God's elect? It is God who justifies, who is he who condemns?" Jesus also said in Matthew 28:18-20 (NKJV), "All authority has been given to Me in heaven and on earth. Go therefore and make disciples of all nations, baptizing them in the name of the Father and of the Son and of the Holy Spirit, teaching them to observe all things that I have commanded you; and lo, I am with you always, even to the end of the age." Amen! Wow! What awesome promises from God! You cannot go wrong when you take God at His Word; everything is stacked in your favor.

With what God has said to Joshua in those first five verses to prepare Joshua, He now says in Joshua 1:6 (NIV), "Be strong and courageous because you will lead these people to inherit the land I swore to their forefathers to give them." Leaders with a divine mantle from God are called to lead others in inheriting what God has promised. As we receive and inherit from God, we will show others how to do the same, as well. It takes strong courage to lead people, because people resist and complain, but you must persevere in what God has called you to do.

Now, God is pressing Joshua even more in verses 7-8. "Be strong and very courageous. Be careful to obey all the law … do not turn from it to the right or left." (Joshua 1:7 NIV). Leaders must press in with courage, and not waver one iota.

"This Book of the Law shall not depart from your mouth, but you shall meditate in it day and night, that you may observe to do according to all that is written in it. For then you will make your way prosperous, and then you will have good success." (Joshua 1:8 NKJV). This verse gives us some basic foundational principles for success. First the Word of God must be in your mouth: you must speak it.

Secondly, you must meditate on the Word of God. That means to review it over and over in your mind. Thirdly, you must obey the Word of God. When you follow this combination, you will prosper in all things in life. If you neglect any of the three, or take shortcuts, it will affect your success.

Three times in this chapter, God instructed Joshua to be strong and full of courage. Also, in Joshua 1:9 (NKJV) God said, "Do not be afraid, nor dismayed, for the Lord your God is with you wherever you go." In other words, do not let trouble or opposition bring you into fear or discouragement. In this chapter God reinforces to Joshua, "I am with you, you will succeed.....But you must prepare yourself to be strong and courageous."

Even though God is on our side and He has given us great and precious promises, there are always struggles that try to take away our faith. But God gave Joshua a great outline for success, so it would be wise for us to take heed as well. Then we too will be successful and prosperous at whatever God calls us to do!

Amen!!!